THE BUSTAN OF SADI

THE BUSTAN OF SADI

TRANSLATED FROM THE PERSIAN
WITH AN INTRODUCTION

by

A. HART EDWARDS

KITAB BHAVAN
NEW DELHI-110002

Kitab Bhavan
Publishers, Distributors, Exporters & Importers
1784, Kalan Mahal, Darya Ganj
New Delhi - 1100 02 (India)

Phone : (91-11) 23277392 / 93, 23274686, 30906494
website : www.kitabbhavan.com
Email : nasri@vsnl.com
Fax : (91-11) 23263383

Edition : 2000
IInd Edition : 2006

ISBN : 81-7151-346-8

Laser Typesetting at :
Laser Track
1784, Kalan Mahal, Darya Ganj
New Delhi-110002 [India]

Published in India by :
Nusrat Ali Nasri for Kitab Bhavan
1784, Kalan Mahal, Darya Ganj
New Delhi - 1100 02 [India]

Printed in India at :
Nice Printing Press
Khureji Khas, Delhi-110051

EDITORIAL NOTE

The object of the Editors of this series is a very definite one. They desire above all things that, in their humble way, these books shall be the ambassadors of goodwill and understanding between East and West—the old world of Thought and the new of Action. In this endeavour, and in their own sphere, they are but followers of the highest example in the land. They are confident that a deeper knowledge of the great ideals and lofty philosophy of Oriental thought may help to a revival of that true spirit of Charity which neither despises nor fears the nations of another creed and colour. Finally, in thanking press and public for the very cordial reception given to the "Wisdom of the East" Series, they wish to state that no pains have been spared to secure the best specialists for the treatment of the various subjects at hand.

L. CRANMER-BYNG

S. A. KAPADIA

CONTENTS

Introduction

INTRODUCTION

If among the twenty-two works with which Sadi enriched the literature of his country the *Gulistan* rank first in popularity, the *Bustan* (lit. "Garden") may justly claim equal precedence in point of interest and merit.

No comprehensive translation of this important classical work has eitherto been placed before the reading public, but it cannot be doubted that the character of its contents is such as to fully instify the attempt now made to familiarize English readers with the entertaining anecdotes and devotional wisdom which the Sage of Shiraz embodied in his Palace of Wealth. This is the name which he applies to the *Bustan* in an introductory chapter, and it is one which springs from something more than a poet's fancy, for the ten doors, or chapters, with which the edifice is furnished lead into a garden that is indeed rich in the fruits of knowledge gained by a wide experience of life in many lands, and earnest thought.

The *Bustan* is written in verse—a fact which adds considerably to the difficulties of translation, since the invariable rule of Sadi, like that of every other Persian poet we have read, is to sacrifice sense to the exigencies of rhyme and metre. In not a few cases the meaning is so confused on this account that even the native commentators, who possess a fund of ingenuity in explaining what they do not properly understand, have been compelled to pass over numerous couplets through sheer inability to unravel their intricacies and the abstruse ideas of the poet.

Probably in no other language in the world is poetic licence so freely permitted and indulged in as in Persian. The construction of sentences follows no rule; the order of words is just that which the individual poet chooses to adopt, and the idea of time—past, present, and future—is ignored in the use of tenses, that part of a verb being alone employed which rhymes the best.

Notwithstanding idiosyncrasies of this kind, the *Bustan* is written in a style that is delightfully pure and admirably adapted to the subject. The devout spirit by which Sadi was characterized throughout his chequered life is revealed in every page of the book. In the *Gulistan* he gave free rein to the quaint humour which for many centuries has been the delight of the Eastern peoples, and which an ever-increasing body of English readers is learning to appreciate and admire. In the *Bustan* the humour is more restrained; its place is taken by a more sober reasoning of the duties of mankind towards the Deity and towards their fellow-men. Devotion to God and the inflexibility of Fate are the underlying texts of every poem, and the ideality of the one and the stern reality of the other are portrayed in language the beauty of which, it is to be feared, the English rendering does not always adequately convey.

The poems abound in metaphor, a figure of style which Eastern writers employ to a degree that is always exaggerated, and sometimes tedious; but for the purpose of this translation, which aims at a happy medium between literal accuracy and the freed requisite in order to render Oriental phraseology into polite English, numerous of the more far-fetched allusions have been discarded, to the benefit of the text.

Although a memoir of Sadi's life is included in another volume of this series, it may not be out of place to give here a brief outline of the poet's career, especially as the *Bustan* contains several references to his childhood and travels.

Sheikh Muslih-ud-din Sadi was born in Shiraz, in Persia, A.D. 1175; that it is to say, 571 years after the flight of Muhammad from Makkah to Madinah. He was the son of one Abdu'llah (servant of God), who held a Government office under the Diwan of that time. Sadi was a child when his father died, as is made clear from the pathetic poem in the second chapter, ending with these words :

Well do I know the orphan's sorrow,
For my father departed in my childhood.

But poorly endowed with earthly riches, Sadi endured many hardships in consequence of this bereavement, and was eventually obliged to live, together with his mother, under the protection of a Saracen chief. How long he remained there it is impossible to say, for the reason that his biographers are the reverse of informing. This much is, however, known, that being imbued from early childhood with an insatiable thirst for knowledge, he eventually journeyed to Baghdad, then at the zenith of its intellectual fame, and was enabled to enter a private school there through the generosity of a wealthy native gentleman. Making full use of the opportunity so favourably presented, the young aspirant progressed rapidly along the path of learning, and at the age of twenty-one made his first essays in authorship. Some fragmentary poems which he submitted with a long dedication to Shams-ud-din, the Professor a Literature at the Nizamiah College of Baghdad, so pleased that able and discerning man that he at once fixed upon Sadi a liberal allowance from his own private purse, with the promise of every further assistance in his power. Soon after this, Said was admitted into the college, and ultimately gained an Idrar, or fellowship. In the seventh chapter of the *Bustan* he narrates an instructive story reminiscent of his studies at Nizamiah, and, prone to conceit though he often is, he tells the story against himself.

His scholastic life did not terminate until he had reached the age of thirty. Of the value of this prolonged period of study he himself was fully cognisant. "Dost thou not know," he asks in the seventh chapter, "how Sadi attained to rank? Neither did he traverse the plains nor journey across the seas. In his youth he lived under the yoke of the wise: God granted him distinction in after-life. And it is not long before he who is submissive in obedience exercises command." No better example of the truth of this passage could be cited than that afforded by his own case.

On leaving Baghdad, he went in company with his tutor, Abdul Qadir Gilani, on a pilgrimage to Makkah.

This was the first of many travels extending over a period of thirty years, in the course of which he visited Europe, India, and practically every part of what are known as the Near and Middle East. A trip through Syria and Turkey is specifically mentioned in this book as inspiring the composition of the *Bustan*. Not wishing, as he tells us, to return empty-handed to his friends at Shiraz, he built the Palace of Wealth, and offered it to them as a gift. He does not conceal the high opinion which he himself placed upon this product of his gifted pen. The gracefully worded phrases with which he predicted the undying popularity of the *Gulistan* finds a parallel in the dedication of the *Bustan* to Atabak Abu Bakr-bin-Sad, the illustrious monarch of Persia beneath whose protection Sadi spent the latter half of his life.

"Although not wishing to sing the praises of kings," he writes, "I have dedicated this book to one so that perhaps the pious will say that Sadi, who surpassed all in eloquence, lived in the time of Abu Bakr Sad." Then, addressing the king, he adds: "Happy is thy fortune that Said's date coincides with thine, for as long as the moon and sun are in the skies thy memory will remain eternal in this book." This conceit is pardonable, since it has been amply justified by time.

After the thirty years of travel, Sadi, becoming elderly, settled down in Persia, where, as has been said, he gained the favour of the rulling prince, from whom he derived not only the dignity and the more tangible advantages of the post of Poet-Laureate, but his takhallus, or titular name, of Sadi. He died at the ripe age of 116, and was buried in his native city.

If the *Bustan* were the only monument that remained of his genius, his name would assuredly still be inscribed in the roll of the Immortals. One feature of his great intellectual faculties needs to be emphasized, and all the more so because it is apt to be overlooked. That is the increasing power which they assumed as he advanced in years, the truth of which can be understood when it is stated that he composed the *Bustan* at the age of 82, the *Bulistan* appearing twelve months later. Few, if any, instances of such sustained mental activity are to be found elsewhere in the entire world's history of letters.

Under the several headings of the various chapters a wide range of ethical subjects is discussed, the whole forming a compendium of moral philosophy the broad principles of which must remain for all time as irrefutable as the precepts of Scriptual teaching.

Sadi's spiritual message is not that of a visionary. His religion was an eminently practical one—he had no sympathies with the recluse and the ascetic. To fulfil one's duties towards one's fellow-men is to fulfil one's duty towards the Deity. That is the root-idea of his teachings. "Religion," he observes, "consists only in the service of the people: it does not lie in the rosary, or prayer-rug, or mendicant's habit."

This couplet, occurring in the opening chapter, is put into the mouth of a certain pious man whom one of the kings of Persia is said to have visited in a repentant mood for the purpose of seeking counsel. The story, like many others in the book, may or may not have any foundation in fact, "the histories of ancient kings," which the poet frequently quotes as his authority, being rather too vague to be convincing. At the same time, the historical allusions form an interesting and instructive background to the legends and the moral precepts so abundantly interwoven among them.

Although Persia is only yet in the process of readjusting her ideas of government and the prerogatives of rulers, principles more advanced than seem compatible with despotism have been for many centuries current among her people, in theory, at least, if not in practice. Muhammad said that a little practice with much knowledge was better than much practice with little knowledge. On that ground Persia has defence, for the knowledge certainly was there. What could better describe the true relationship between king and people than Sadi's thirteenth-century epigram?—

Subjects are as the root and the king is as the tree.
And the tree, O son, gains strength from the root.

In 1910 the autocratic tree at Teheran was rudely severed from its root; perchance the successors of Abu Bakr were not of those to whom "the words of Sadi are agreeable."

The saving grace of benevolence is illustrated in the second chapter by means of some entertaining anecdotes, of two of which the hero is Hatim Tai, the famous Arabian chief, whose generosity was such that he preferred to die rather than disappoint the messenger sent by a jealous king to slay him. The story of the

Darwesh and the Fox is noteworthy inasmuch as it throws a much-needed light upon the Eastern interpretation of all that is implied by "qismat." It is commonly supposed that the sense of inevitability removes from the Eastern's mind the necessity for individual effort. This view is distinctly erroneous. No such pernicious doctrine is, at any rate, subscribed to by the educated classes; to the lazy and ne'er-do-well who plead Fate as their excuse, Sadi points the moral.

After demonstrating in the two succeeding chapters the powerlessness of man to avert the decrees of Fate, and the virtues of contentment, the poet passes on to discuss the cultivation of the mind. The comparison here drawn between the human mind and a city "full of good and evil desires," of which the Ego is the Sultan and Reason the Vazier, is original and full of meaning. Despite his own much-vaunted eloquence and facility of speech, Sadi condemns in scathing terms the man of many words, remarking poignantly that "a grain of musk is better than a heap of mud." So, too, in his opinion, is a thief better than a backbiter, and, apropos of the gentler sex, a woman of good nature better than one of beauty. The advice to take a new wife every year cannot be regarded seriously, even though it be true that last year's almanace has lost its usefulness. More worthy of the poet is the discourse on the training of children. Nothing truer than the sentiments expressed in this poem did he ever utter, and in England today there can be few who would dispute them.

Excessive charm pervades the three concluding chapters. If that bigotry and spirit of intolerance of which the Mussalman, no less than the followers of other creeds, is guilty is revealed in no small measures, criticism on that score must give place to wonder and admiration for the sincere and perfervid homage which the poet renders to the Deity whom, in the essence, all nations worship.

The narrative, in the eighth chapter, of Sadi's adventure with the idolaters in Guzerat will be found amusing as well as enlightening.

Nothing now remains for the translator but to join with Sadi in his plea for indulgent criticism :

Never have I heard it said
The wise found fault with what they read,
Though of Chiness cloth a robe be made,
Inside must a cotton lining be laid.
If thou wouldst but the cloth, seek not to condemn—
Gloss over the cotton with acumen.
On the Day of Judgement the wicked will be
Forgiven, through them that have purity.
If in my words thou evil find,
Do likewise, forgive, for more is behind.
If a word in a thousand suit thy taste,
Do not denounce the rest in haste.

The poet goes on to remark that his compositions are esteemed in Persia as is the choicest musk of Tartary: the translator is less fortunate and more modest.

A.H.E.

THE BUSTAN OF SADI

PROLOGUE

In the Name of God, the Compassionate, the Merciful

In the name of Him Who created and sustains the world, the Sage Who endowed tongue with speech.

He attains no honour who turns the face from the doer of His mercy.

The Kings of the earth prostrate themselves before Him in supplication.

He seizes not in haste the disobedient, nor drives away the penitent with violence. The two worlds are as a drop of water in the ocean of His knowledge.

He withholds not His bounty though His servants sin; upon the surface of the earth has He spread a feast, in which both friend and foe may share.

Peerless He is, and His kingdom is eternal. Upon the head of one He pleceth a crown another he hurleth from the throne to the ground.

The fire of His friend He turneth into a flower garden; through the waters of the Nile He sendeth His foes to perdition.

Behind the veil He seeth all, and concealeth our faults with His own goodness.

He is near to them that are downcast, and accepteth the prayers of them that lament.

He knoweth of the things that exist not, of secrets that are untold.

He causeth the moon and the sun to revolve, and spreadeth water upon the earth.

In the heart of a stone hath He placed a jewel; from nothing hath He created all that is.

Who can reveal the secret of His qualities; what eye can see the limits of His beauty?

The bird of thought cannot soar to the height of His presence, nor the hand of understanding reach to the skirt of His praise.

Think not, O Sadi, that one can walk in the road of purity except in the footsteps of Muhammad.

He is the patriarch of the prophets, the guide of the path of salvation; the mediator of mankind, and the chief of the Court of Judgement. What of thy praises can Sadi utter? The mercy of God be upon thee, O Prophet, and peace!

On the Reason for the Writing of the Book

I travelled in many regions of the globe and passed the days in the company of many men. I reaped advantages in every corner, and gleaned an ear of corn from every harvest. But I saw none like the pious and devout men of Shiraz—upon which land be the grace of God—my attachment with whom drew away my heart from Syria and Turkey.

I regretted that I should go from the garden of the world empty-handed to my friends, and reflected: "Travellers bring sugarcandy from Egypt as a present to their friends. Although I have no candy, yet have I words that are sweeter. The sugar that I bring is not that which is eaten, but what knowers of truth take away with respect."

When I built this Palace of Wealth,[1] I furnished it with ten doors of instruction.[2]

It was in the year 655 that this famous treasury became full of the pearls of eloquence. A quilted robe of silk, or of Chiness embroidery, must of necessity be padded with cotton; if thou obtain aught of the silk, fret not—be generous and conceal the cotton. I have heard that in the day of Hope and Fear the Merciful One will pardon the evil for the sake of the good. If thou see evil in my words, do thou likewise. If one couplet among a thousand please thee, generously withhold thy fault finding.

Assuredly, my compositions are esteemed in Persia as the priceless musk of Khutan. Sadi brings roses to the garden with mirth. His verses are like dates encrusted with sugar—when opened, a stone[3] is revealed inside.

Concerning Atabak Abu Bakr, son of Sad[4]

Although not desiring to write in praise of kings, I have inscribed this book to the name of a certain one so

---

1. *I.e.* the *Bustan*.
2. *I.e.*, its ten chapters.
3. Lit. "bone" used metaphorically in the sense of "a truth."
4. One of the kings of Persia in whose reign Sadi flourished. His full name was Atãbak Muzaffar-ud-Din Abû Bakr-bin-Sa'd-bin-Zangî.

that perhaps the pious may say: "Sadi, who surpassed all in eloquence, lived in the time of Abu Bakr, the son of Sad." Thus, in this book will his memory remain so long as the moon and sun are in the skies. Beyond count are his virtues—may the world fulfil his desires, the heavens be his friend, and the Creator be his guardian.

CHAPTER I

Concerning Justice, Counsel, and the Administration of Government

The goodness of God surpasseth imagination; what service can the tongue of praise perform?

Keep, O God, this king,[1] Abu Bakr, beneath whose shadow is the protection of the people, long established upon his throne, and make his heart to live in obedience to Thee. Render fruitful his tree of hope; prolong his youth, and adorn his face with mercy.

O King! deck not thyself in royal garments when thou comest to worship: make thy supplications like a darwesh, saying: "O God! powerful and strong Thou art. I am no monarch, but a beggar in Thy court. Unless Thy help sustain me, what can issue from my hand? Succour me, and give me the means of virtue, or else how can I benefit my people?"

If thou rule by day, pray fervently by night. The great among thy servants wait upon thee at thy door; thus shouldest thou serve, with thy head in worship upon God's threshold.

Nushiravan's[2] Counsel to His Son

---

1. *I.e.* Abû Bakr.
2. Naushîravãn the Just was the twentieth king of the fourth dynasty of Persia, and contemporary with the Roman Emperor Justinian. The Prophet Muhammad was born in his reign.

Thus, when at the point of death, did Nushiravan counsel his son Hurmuz :

"Cherish the poor, and seek not thine own comfort. The shephered should not sleep while the wolf is among the sheep. Protect the needy, for a king wears his crown for the sake of his subjects. The people are as the root and the king is as the tree; and the trcc, O son, gains strength from the root. He should not oppress the people who has fear of injury to his kingdom. Seek not plenteousness in that land where the people are afflicted by the king. Fear them that are proud and them that fear not God."

Discourse Concerning Travellers

The king who deals harshly with merchants who come from after closes the door of well-being upon the whole of his subjects. When do the wise return to the land of which they hear rumours of bad custom?

If thou desire a good name, hold merchants and travellers in high esteem, for they carry they reputation through the world. Be cautious also lest, being enemies in the guise of friends, they seek thy injury.

Advance the dignities of old friends, for treachery comes not from them that are cherished.

When thy servant becomes stricken in years, be not unmindful of the obligations towards him. If old age binds his hand from service, the land of generosity yet remains to thee.

Story Illustrating the Need for Deliberation

There once landed at a seaport of Arabia a man who had widely travelled and was versed in many sciences. He presented himself at the palace of the king, who was so captivated by his wisdom and knowledge that he appointed the traveller to the raziership.

With such skill did he perform the duties of that office that he offended none, and brought the kingdom completely beneath his sway. He closed the mouths of slanderers, because nothing evil issued from his hand; and the envious, who could detect no fault in him, bemoaned their lack of opportunity to do him injury.

At the court, however, there were two beautiful young slaves towards whom the vazier displayed no small measure of affection. (If thou wouldst that thy rank endure, incline not thy heart towards the fair; and though thy love be innocent, have care, for there is fear of loss).

The former vazier, who had been dismissed to make room for the newcomer, maliciously carried the story to the king.

"I know not," he said, "who this new minister may be, but he lives not chastely in this hand. I have heard that he intrigues with two of thy slaves—he is a perfidious man, and lustful. It is not right that one such as he should bring ill-fame upon the court. I am not so unmindful of the favours that I have received at thy hands that I should see these things and remains silent."

Angered by what he heard, the king stealthily watched the new Wazier, and when, later, he observed the latter glance towards one of the slaves, who returned a covert smile, his suspicious of evil became at once confirmed.

Summoning the minister to his side, he said: "I did not know thee to be shameless and unworthy. Such lofty station is not thy proper place. But the fault is mine. If I cherish one who is of evil nature, assuredly do I sanction disloyalty in my house."

"Since my skirt is free from guilt," the vazier replied, "I fear not the malignity of the evil-wisher. I know not who has accused me of what I have not done."

"This was told me by the old vazier," explained the king.

The vazier smiled and said, "Whatever he said is no cause for wonder. What would the envious man say when he saw me in his former place? Him I knew to be my enemy that day when Khasrav[1] appointed him to lower rank than me. Never till Doomsday will he accept me as a friend when in my promotion he sees his own decline. If thou wilt give ear to thy slave I will narrate a story that is apropos.

"In a dream someone saw the Prince of Evil, whose figure was as erect as a fire-tree, and whose face was as fair as the sun. Regarding him, the sleeper said: 'O splendid being! Mankind knows not of thy beauty. Fearful of countenance do they imagine thee, and hideous have they depicted thee on the walls of the public baths.

---

1. A title of the king of Persia. It was originally applied to Naushîravãn.

The Prince of Evil smiled: 'Such is not my figure, he replied; 'but the pencil was in the hand of an enemy! The root of their stock did I throw out of Paradise; now in malice do they paint me ugly.'

"In the same way," continued the vazier, "although my fame is good, the envious speak ill of me. Those who are guiltless are brave in speech; only he who gives false weight has fear of the inspector."

"Forsooth," the king exclaimed, his anger rising, "I heard this not only from thine enemy. Have I not seen with my own eyes that among the assemblage of this court thou regardest none but those two slaves?"

"That is true," the vazier said, "but I will explain this matter if thou wilt listen. Dost thou not know that the beggar eyes the rich with envy? Once, like those slaves, did I possess both grace and beauty. Two rows of teeth were set behind my lips, erect like a wall of ivory[1] brîcks. One by one, like ancient bridges, have they fallen—regard me now as here I stand! Why may I not glance with envy at those slaves when they recall to me the past?

When the wise man had pierced this pearl of lustrous truth, the king exclaimed : "Better than this it would be impossible to speak. Permissible it is to look toward the fair is one who can thus excuse himself. Had I not in wisdom acted with deliberation, I should have wronged him through the speech of an enemy."

1. Lit. "silver."

To carry the hand quickly to the sword in anger is to carry the back of the hand to the teeth in regret. Head not the words of the envious; if thou actest upon them, remorseful wilt thou be.

Admonishing the slanderer for his evil words, the king further increased the dignity of the vazier, who directed the affairs of the State for many years with justice and benevolence, and was long remembered for his virtues.

Story of the King Whose Coat was Coarse

A certain just king habitually wore a coat of coarse material. Someone said to him: "O happy king! Make for thyself a coat of Chinese brocadc."

"That which I wear," the king replied, "affords both covering and comfort; anything beyond that is luxury. I collect not tribute that I may adorn my person and my throne. If, like a woman, I ornament my body, how, like a man, can I repulse the enemy? The royal treasuries are not for me alone—they are filled for the sake of the army, not for the purchase of ornaments and jewellery."

Story of Darius[1] and the Herdsman

Darius, king of Persia, became separated from his retinue while hunting. A herdsman came running towards

1. Darius Codomanus was the last king of Persia. He waged many wars with Alexander the Great, who finally defeated him at Arbela. The unfortunate king was afterwards killed by one Bessus, governor of Bactriana, 331 B.C.

him, and the king assuming the man to be an enemy, adjusted his bow. Thereupon the herdsman cried: "I am no enemy; seek not to kill me. I am he who tends the king's horses, and in this meadow am thus engaged."

Becoming again composed, the king smiled and said: "Heaven has befriended thee; otherwise would I have drawn the bowstring to my ear."

"It showeth neither wise administration nor good judgment," replied the herdsman, "when the king knows not an enemy from a friend. Those who are greatest should know those who are least. Many times hast thou seen me in thy presence, and asked of me concerning the horses and the grazing-fields. Now that I come again before thee thou takest me for an enemy. More skilled am I, O king, for I can distinguish one horse out of a hundred thousand. Tend thou thy people as I, with sense and judgment tend my horses."

Ruin brings sorrow to that kingdom where the wisdom of the shephered exceeds that of the king.

Story of Abdul Aziz and the Pearl

The story is told of Abdul Aziz that he had a pearl of great beauty and value set in a ring. Shortly after, a severe drought occurred, causing distress among the people. Moved by compassion, the king ordered the pearl to be sold and the money that it fetched to be given to the poor.

Someone chided him for doing this, saying: "Never again will such a stone come into thy hands."

Weeping, the king replied: "Ugly is an ornament upon the person of a king when the hearts of his people are distressed by want. Better for me is a stoneless ring than a sorrowing people."

Happy is he who sets the ease of others above his own. The virtuous desire not their own pleasure at the expense of others. When the king sleeps neglectfully upon him couch, I trow not that the beggar finds enviable repose.

Story of How Tukla was Rebuked by a Devotee

Tukla, king of Persia, once visited a devotee and said: "Fruitless have been my years. None but the beggar carries riches from the world when earthly dignities are passed. Hence, would I now sit in the corner of devotion that I might usefully employ the few short days that yet remain to me."

The devotee was angered at these words.

"Enough!" he cried. "Religion consists alone in the service of the people; it finds no place in the rosary, or prayer-rug, or tattered garment. Be a king in sovereignty and a devotee in purity of morals. Action, not words, is demanded by religion, for words without action are void of substance."

Discourse Concerning Riches and Poverty

Say not that no dignity excels that of sovereignty, for no kingdom is more free from care than that of the darwesh.

They that are the most lightly burdened reach the destination first.

The poor man is afflicted by lack of bread the king by the cares of his kingdom.

Though one may rule and another may serve, though the one be exalted to the height of Saturn and the other languish in a prison, when death has claimed them it will not be possible to distinguish between the two.

Story of Qazal Arsalan[1] and the Fort

Qazal Arsalan possessed a fort, which raised its head to the height of Alwand.[2] Secure from all were those within its walls, for its roads were a labyrinth, like the curls of a bride.

From a learned traveller Qazal once inquired : "Didst thou ever, in thy wanderings, see a fort as strong as this?"

"Splendid it is," was the reply, "but methinks not it confers much strength. Before thee, did not other kings possess it for a while, then pass away? After thee, will not other kings assume control, and eat the fruits of the tree of thy hope?"

In the estimation of the wise, the world is a false gem that passes each moment from one hand to another.

---

1. One of the kings of Persia. He was called Qazal because of the redness of his hair. Arsalãn means "a lion."
2. Name of a lofty mountain situated in Hamdãn north-west of Isfahãn.

A Story of Damascus

Such famine was there once in Damascus that lovers forgot their love. So miserly was the sky towards the earth that the sown fields and the date-trees moistened not their lips. Fountains dried up, and no water remained but the tears in the eyes of the orphans. If smoke issued from a chimney, nought was it but the sighs of the widows. Like beggars, the trees stood leafless, and the mountains lost their verdure. The locusts devoured the gardens, and men devoured the locusts.

At that time came to me a friend on whose bones skin alone remained. I was astonished, since he was of lofty rank and rich. "O friend!" said I, "what misfortune has befallen thee?"

"Where is thy sense?" he answered. "Seest thou not that the severities of famine have reached their limit? Rain comes not from the sky, neither do the lamentations of the suffering reach to heaven."

"Thou, at least," I urged, "hast nought to fear; poison kills only where there is no antidote."

Regarding me with indignation, as a learned man regards a fool, my friend replied: "Although a man be safely on the shore, he stands not supine while his friends are drowning. My face is not pale through want; the sorrows of the poor have wounded my heart. Although, praise be to Allah, I am free from wounds, I tremble when I see the wounds of others."

Bitter are the pleasures of him who is in health when a sick man is at his side. When the beggar has not eaten, poisonous and baneful is one's food.

Story of a Bully

A bully fell down a well and passed the night in wailing and lamenting. Someone threw a stone down on to his head, and said: "Didst thou ever go to any one's assistance that thou shouldest today cry out for help? Didst thou ever sow the seeds of virtue? Who would place a salve upon thy wounds when the hearts of all cry out by reason of thy tyrannies? Across our path thou didst dig a pit, into which, perforce, hast thou now fallen."

If thou do evil expect not goodness; never does the withered grape-wine bring forth fruit;

O thou who soweth the seed in autumn! I think not that thou wilt reap the corn at harvest-time.

If thou nourish the thorn-tree of the desert, think not that thou wilt ever eat its fruit.

Green dates come not from the poisonous colocynth; when thou sowest seed, hope only for the fruit of that very seed.

CHAPTER II

Concerning Benevolence

If Thou art wise, incline towards the essential truth, for that remains, while the things that are external pass away.

He who as neither knowledge, generosity, nor piety resembles a man in form alone.

He sleeps at peace beneath the ground who made tranquil the hearts of men.

Give now of thy gold and bounty, for eventually will it pass from thy grasp. Open the door of thy treasure today, for tomorrow the key will not be in thy hands.

If thou would not be distressed on the Day of Judgment, forget not them that are distressed.

Drive not the poor man empty from thy door, lest thou should wander before the doors of strangers.

He protects the needy who fears that he himself may become needful of the help of others.

Art not thou, too, a supplicant? Be grateful, and turn not away them that supplicate thee.

Story Illustrative of Doing Good to the Evil

A woman said to her husband : Do not again buy bread from the baker in this street. Make thy purchases in the market, for this man shows wheat and sells barely,[1] and he has no customers but a warm of flies."

"O light of my life," the husband answered, "Pay no heed to his trickery. In the hope of our custom has he settled in this place, and not humane would it be to deprive him of his profits.

Follow the path of the righteous, and, if thou stand upon thy feet, stretch out thy hand to them that are fallen.

Story Concerning Fasting

The wife of an officer of a king said to her husband: "Arise, and go to the royal palace, thai they may give thee food, for thy children are in want."

"The kitchen is closed today," he answered; "last night the Sultan resolved to fast awhile."

In the despair of hunger, the woman bowed her head and murmured : "What does the Sultan seek from his fasting when his breaking the fast means a festival of joy for our children?"

One who eats that good may follow is better than a Mammon-worshipper who continually fasts. Proper it is to fast with him who feeds the needy in the morning.

Story Illustrative of Practical Charity

A certain man had generosity without the means of displaying it; his pittance was unequal to his

---

1.*I.e.* shows one thing and sells another of inferior quantity. The expression is commonly used to denote a hypocrite.

benevolence. (May riches never fall to the mean, nor poverty be the lot of the generous!) His charities exceeding the depth of his pocket, therefore was he always short of money.

One day a poor man wrote to him saying : "O thou of happy nature! Assist me with funds, since for some time have I languished in prison.

The generous man would have willingly acceded to the request, but he possessed not so much as the smallest piece of money. But he sent someone to the creditors of the prisoner with the message: "Free this man for a few days, and I will be his security."

Then did he visit the prisoner in his cell and say: "Arise, and fly with haste from the city.

When a sparrow sees open the door of its cage, it tarries not a moment. Like the morning breeze, the prisoner flew from the land. Thereupon, they seized his benefactor, saying: "Produce either the man or the money."

Powerless to do either, he went to prison, for a bird escaped is ne'er recaught. Long there did he remain, invoking help from none, nor complaining, though he slept not at nights through restlessness.

A pious man came to gim and said: "I did not think that thou wert dishonest; why art thou here imprisoned?"

"No villainy have I committed," he replied. "I saw a helpless man in bonds and his freedom only in my own confinement. I did not deem it right that I should live in comfort while another was fettered by the legs."

Eventually he died, leaving a good name behind.

Happy is he whose name dies not! He who sleeps beneath the earth with a heart that lives is better that he who lives with a soul that is dead, for the former remains for ever.

Story of Man and a Thirsty Dog

In a desert a man found a dog that was dying from thirst. Using his hat as a bucket, he fetched water from a well and gave it to the helpless animal. The prophet of the time stated that God had forgiven the man his sins because of his kindly act.

Reflect, if thou be a tyrant, and make a profession of benevolence.

He who shows kindness to a dog will not do less towards the good among his fellows.

Be generous to the extent of thy power. If thou hast not dug a well in the desert, at least place a lamp in a shrine.[1]

Charity distributed from an ox's skin that is filled with treasure counts for less than a dinar given from the wages of toil.

Every man's burden is suited to his strength—heavy to the ant is the foot of the locust.

---

1. To do either is considered an act of virtue among Muhammadans.

Do good to others so that on the morrow God may not deal harshly with thee.

Be lenient with thy slave, for he may one day become a king, like a pawn that becomes a queen.

Story Apropos of Nemesis

A poor man complained of his distressed condition to one who was rich as well as ill-dispostioned. The latter refused to help him, and turned roughly upon him in anger.

The beggar's heart bled by reason of this violence: "Strange!" he reflected, "that this rich man should be of such forbidding countenance! Perhaps he fears not the bitterness of begging."

The rich man ordered his slave to drive the beggar away. As a result of his ingratitude for the blessings that he enjoyed, Fortune forsook him, and he lost all that he possessed. His slave passed into the hands of a generous man of enlightened mind, who was as gladdened at the sight of a beggar as the latter is at the sight of riches.[1]

One night a beggar asked alms of the latter, and he commanded his slave to give the man to eat. When the slave took food to the supplicant he involuntarily uttered a cry, and went back weeping.

"Why these tears?" his master asked.

"My heart is grieved at the plight of this unfortunate old man," the slave replied. "Once was he the owner of much wealth, and I his slave."

---

1. By reason of the opportunity it presented to bestow his charity.

The master smiled and said: "This is not cause for grief, O son. Time, in its revolutions, is not unjust. Was not that indigent man formerly a merchant who carried his head high in the air through pride? I am he whom that day he drove from his door. Fate has now put him in the place that I then occupied. Heaven befriended me and washed the dust of sorrow from my face. Though God, in His wisdom, closed one door, another, in His mercy, did He open."

Many a needy one has become filled, and many a Plutos has gone empty.

Story of a Fool and a Fox

Someone saw a fox that was bereft of the use of its legs. He was wondering how the animal managed to live in this condition when a tiger drew near with a jackal in its claws. The tiger ate the jackal, and the fox finished the remains. The next day also did the Omnipotent Provider send the fox its daily meal.

The eyes of the man were thus opened to the light of true knowledge. "After this," he reflected, "I will sit in a corner like an ant, for the elephant's portion is not gained by reason of its strength."

So did he sit in silence, waiting for his daily food to come from the Invisible. No one heeded him, and soon was he reduced to skin and bones. When, at last, his senses had almost gone through weakness, a voice came out from the wall of a mosque, saying :

"Go, O false one! Be the rending tiger, and pose not as a paralytic fox. Exert thyself like the tiger, so that something may remain from thy spoil. Why, like the fox, appease thy hunger with leaving? Eat of the fruits of thine own endeavours; strive like a man, and relieve the wants of the needy."

Seize, O youth, the hand of the aged; fall not thyself, saying, "Hold my hand." In the two words does he obtain reward who does good to the people of God.

Story of a Devout Miser

In the remote regions of Turkey there lived a good and pious man, whom I and some fellow-travellers once visited. He received us cordially, and seated us with respect. He had vineyards, and wheat-fields, slaves and gold, but was as miserly as a leafless tree. His feelings were warm, but his fireplace was cold. He passed the night awake in prayer, and we in hunger. In the morning he girt his loins and recommenced the same politeness of the previous night.

One of our party was of merry wit and temper. "Come, give us food in change for a kiss,"[1] he said, "for that is better to a hungry man. In serving me, place not thy hand upon my shoe, but give me bread and strike thy shoe upon my head."

Excellence is attained by generosity, not by vigils in the night.

---

1. It is impossible to convey the beauty of this line in English. The Persian words here used to express "food" and "kiss" are written alike, except for one diacritical mark, and the word "change" literally means "making an error in writing and changing the diacritical points."

Idle words are a hollow drum; invocations without merit are a weak support.

Story of Hatim Tai[1]

Hatim Tai possessed a horse whose fleetness was as that of the morning breeze. Of this was the Sultan of Turkey informed.

"Like Hatim Tai," he was told, "none is equal in generosity; like his horse, nothing is equal in speed and gait. As a ship in the sea it traverses the desert, while the eagle, exhausted, lags behind."

"From Hatim will I request that horse," the king replied. "If he be generous and give it to me, then shall I know that his fame is true; if not, that it is but the sound of a hollow drum."

So he despatched a messenger with ten followers to Hatim. They alighted at the house of the Arab chief, who prepared a feast and killed a horse[2] in their honour.

On the following day, when the messenger explained the object of his mission, Hatim became as one mad with grief. "Why," he cried, "didst thou not give me before thy message? That swift-paced horse did I roast last night for thee to eat. No other means had I to enterain thee; that horse alone stood by my tent, and I would not that my guests should sleep fasting."

1. Hatim Tai was an Arabian chief who was renowned for his generosity. He was born in Yaman, in Arabia Felix, and lived some time before Muhammad in the six century. Many legends have been woven round his life and character.

2. Horse-flesh was formerly eaten in parts of the East.

To the men he gave money and splendid robes, and when the news of his generosity reached to Turkey, the king showered a thousand praises upon his nature.

Story of Hatim and the Messenger Sent to Kill Him

One of the kings of Yaman was renowned for his liberality, yet the name of Hatim was never mentioned in his presence without his falling into a rage. "How long," he would ask, "wilt thou speak of that vain man, who possesses neither a kingdom, nor power, nor wealth?"

On one occasion he prepared a royal feast, which the people were invited to attend. Someone began to speak of Hatim, and another to praise him. Envious, the king despatched a man to slay the Arabian chief, reflecting: "So long as Hatim lives, my name will never become famous."

The messenger departed, and travelled far seeking for Hatim that he might kill him. As he went along the road a youth came out to meet him. He was handsome and wise, and showed friendliness toward the messenger, whom he took to his house to pass the night. Such liberality did he shower upon his guest that the heart of the evil-minded one was turned to goodness.

In the morning the generous youth kissed his hand and said : "Remain with me for a few days."

"I am unable to tarry here," replied the messenger, "for urgent business is before me."

"If thou wilt entrust me with thy secret," said the youth, "to aid thee will I spare no effort."

"O generous man!" was the reply, "give ear to me, for I know that the generous are concealers of secrets. Perhaps in this country thou knowest Hatim, who is of lofty mind and noble qualities. The king of Yaman desires his head, though I know not what enmity has arisen between them. Grateful shall I be if thou wilt direct me to where he is. This hope from thy kindness do I entertain, O friend!".

The youth laughed and said: "I am Hatim; see here my head! strike it from my body with thy sword. I would not that harm should befall thee, or that thou shouldest fall in thy endeavour."

Throwing aside his sword, the man fell on the ground and kissed the dust of Hatim's feet. "If I injured a hair on thy body," he cried, "I should no longer be a man." So saying, he clasped Hatim to his breast and took his way back to Yaman.

"Come," said the king as the man approached, "what news hast thou? Why didst thou not tie his head to thy saddle-straps? Perhaps that famous one attacked thee and thou wert too weak to engage in combat."

The messenger kissed the ground and said: "O wise and just king! I found Hatim, and saw him to be generous and full of wisdom, and in courage superior to myself. My back was bent by the burden of his favours; with the sword of kindness and bounty he killed me."

When he had related all that he had seen of Hatim's generosity, the king uttered praises upon the family of the Arab chief and rewarded the messenger with gold.

Story Illustrative of Misdirected Kindness

A certain man, in the ceiling of whose house some bees had built their hives, asked his wife for a butcher's knife so that he might destroy them. "Do not so," the woman said, "for the poor creatures will be greatly distressed when turned out of their homes."

Accordingly, the foolish man left the bees in peace.

One day the woman was stung by one of the insects and stood wailing on the doorstep. Hearing her cries the husband left his shop and hurried towards the house. Angered, he said: "O wife! show not such a bitter face to the world; remember thou didst say to me, 'Kill not the poor bees.'"

How can onc do good to the evil? Forbearance with the wicked but increase their iniquity:

What is a dog that a dish of viands should be set before him? Command that they should give him bones. A kicking animal is best well-burdened.

If the night-watchman display humanity, no one sleeps at night for fear of thieves.

In the battlefield, the spear-shaft is worth more than a hundred thousand sugarcanes.

When thou rearest a cat, she destroys thy pigeons; when thou makest fat a wolf, he rends one who is dear to thee.

Raise not a building that has not a strong foundation; if thou dost, beware.

Discourse Concerning Kindness to Orphans

Protect him whose father is dead; remove the dust from his raiment, and injure him not. Thou knowest not how hard is his condition; no foliage is there on a rootless tree. Give not a kiss to a child of thine own in the sight of a helpless orphan. If the latter weep, who will assuage his grief? If he be angered, who will bear his burden? See that he weeps not, for the throne of God trembles at the orphan's lament. With pity, wipe the tears from his eyes and the dust from his face. If the protecting shadow of his father's care be gone, cherish him beneath the shadow of thy care.

Upon my head was a kingly crown when it repose upon the bosom of my father. Then, if a fly settled upon my body, many were distressed on my behalf. Now; should I be taken in captivity, not one among my friends would come to aid me. Well do I know the orphan's sorrow, for my father departed in my childhood.

CHAPTER III

Concerning Love

Happy are the days of them that are infatuated by love for Him, whether they be sorrowed by separation from Him or made joyous by His presence.

They are mendicants who fly from worldly sovereignty; in the hope of meeting Him they are patient in their mendacity. Oft have they drunk of the wine of anguish; be it bitter, they remain silent. In the remembrance of Him patience is not bitter, for wormwood is sweet from the hand of a friend.

They that are captive in the coils of His love, seek not to escape; they suffer reproach, but are monarchs in the seclusion of their meditation, and their way is not known. They are like the temple of Jerusalem, splendid of which is the interior, but whose outer wall is left in ruin.

Like moths, they burn themselves in the fire of love. Their beloved is in their breasts, yet do they seek Him; though near a fountain, their lips are parched.[1]

Discourse Concerning Constancy

Thy love renders thee impatient and disturbed. With such sincerity has thou placed thy head at her feet that thou art oblivious to the world.

---

1. *I.e.* their love for God is insatiable.

When in the eyes of thy beloved riches count not, gold and dust are as one to thee.

Thou sayest that she dwelleth in thine eyes—if they be closed, she is in thy mind.

If she demand thy life, thou dost place it in her hand; if she place a sword upon thy head, thou holdest it forward.

When earthly love produces such confusion and such obedience demands, dost thou wonder if travellers of the road of God remain engulfed in the Ocean of Reality?

In the remembrance of their Friend they have turned their backs upon the world; they are so fascinated by the Cup-bearer that they have spilled the wine.

No medicine can cure them, for no one has knowledge of their pains.

With their cries of longing do they root up a mountain; with their sighs they dismember a kingdom.

Such is their weeping at dawn that the tears wash the collyrium of sleep from their eyes. Night and day are they immersed in the sea of love; so distracted are they that they know not night from day.

So enamoured are they of the beauty of the Painter that they care not for the beauty of His designs.

He drinks of the pure wine of Unity who is forgetful of both this world and the next.

Story of a Dancer

I have heard that, at the singing of a musician, one of fairy-fach began to dance. Surrounded by distracted hearts, the flame of a candle caught her skirt. She was distressed and angered.

One of her lovers said, "Why agitate thyself? The fire has burned thy skirts—it[1] has entirely consumed the harvest of my life."

Story Illustrating the Reality of Love

One who loved God set his face towards the desert. His father, being grieved at his absence, neither ate nor slept.

Someone admonished the son, who said: "Since my Friend has claimed me as His own, no other friendship do I own. When He revealed to me His beauty, all else that I saw appeared unreal."

They that love Him care for no one else; their senses are confused and their ears and deaf to the words of them that reproach.

They wander through the desert of Divine Knowledge without a caravan.

They have no hope of approbation from their fellow-men, for they are the chosen of the elect of God.

Story Illustrative of Patience

An old man begged at the door of a mosque. Someone said to him : "This is not the place to beg; stand not here with impudence."

---

1. *I.e.* the fire of love.

"What house is this," the man inquired, "from which no pity comes upon the condition of the poor?"

"Silence"' was the reply. "What foolish words are these! This is the house of our Master!"

The beggar raised a cry: "Alas," he said, "that I should be disappointed at this door. I have not gone hopeless from any street; why should I go thus from the door of God? Here will I stretch forth my hand of want, for I know that I shall not depart empty-handed."

For a year he remained devoutly employed in the mosque. One night, through weakness, his heat began to palpitate, and at daybreak his last breath flickered like a morning lamp. Thus did he exclaim with joy: "And whoever knocked at the door of the Bounteous One, it opened."

He who seeks God should be patient and enduring; I have not heard of an alchemist being sad. Much gold he reduces to ashes so that he may one day turn copper into gold. Gold is good with which to buy— and what coldest thou wish to buy better than the face of thy Friend?[1]

Story of One Who was Assiduous in Prayer

An old man spent the night in worship and the morning in prayer. A guardian angel whispered to him:

1. "Gold" refers to "life," and "Friend" to "God." The meaning is that one should devote one's life to religion, and thus gain an entrance to the presence of the Deity.

"Go, take thy way, for thy prayers are not acceptable at this door."

The next night again he passed the night in devotion; and a disciple, being informed of his circumstances, said: "When thou seest that the door is shut, why dost thou thus exert thyself?"

Weeping, he replied: "O my son! Dost thou suppose that although He has torn my reins I shall keep my hands from off his saddle-straps? when a supplicant is repelled at one door, what is his fear if he know of another?"

While thus he spoke, with his head upon the ground, the angel uttered this message in his ears: "Although there is no merit in him, his prayers are accepted, for except Me he has no refuge."

Story of Sultan Mahmud and his Love for Ayaz

Someone found fault with the king of Ghazani, saying: "Ayaz, his favourite slave, possesses no beauty. It is strange that a night ingale should love a rose that has neither colour nor perfume."

This was told to Mahmud, who said: "My love, O sir, is for his virtues, nor for his form and stature."

I have heard that in a narrow pass a camel fell and a chest of pearls was broken. The king gave the signal for plunder, and urged on his horse with speed. The horsemen did likewise, and, leaving the king behind, gathered up the pearls, No one of them remained near the king but Ayaz.

"O thou of curly locks!" said Mahmud, "what hast thou gained of the plunder?"

"Nothing," he replied. "I walked in haste behind thee: I do not occupy myself with riches away from thy service."

If an honourable place in the court be thine, be not neglectful of the king on account of gain elsewhere.

Story of a Village Chief

A village chief passed with his son through the centre of the imperial army. In the presence of such pomp and splendour the man displayed humility and fled, through fear, into a corner.

"After all," observed his son, "thou art a village chief, and in chieftaincy greater than the nobles. Why dost thou tremble like a willow tree?"

"True," replied his father. I am a chief and a ruler, but my honour lies as far as my village."

Thus are the saints overwhelmed with fear when they stand in the court of their king.

Story of a Fire-Fly

Perhaps thou mayset have seen the fire-fly shine like a lamp in the garden at night.

"O night-illuminating moth!" someone said, "why comest thou not out in the day time?"

The fly gave an answer full of wisdom: "Because I am not visible before the sun."

Story of a Moth and a Candle

Someone said to a moth: "God, thou contemptible creature, and make friendship with one worthy of thyself; go where thou seest the path of hope. How different is thy love from that of the candle! Thou art not a salamdander—hover not around the fire, for bravery is necessary before combat. It is not compatible with reason that thou shouldest acknowledge as a friend one whom thou knowest to be thine enemy."

"What does it matter if I burn?", the moth replied. "I have love in my heart, and this flame is as a flower to me. Not of my own accord do I throw myself into the fire; the chain of her love is upon my neck. Who is it that finds fault with my friendship of my friend? I am content to be slain at her feet. I burn because she is dear to me, and because my destruction may affect her. So not to the helpless man from whose hands the reins have fallen, 'Drive slowly."

Another Story on the Same Subject

One night, as I lay awake, I heard a moth say to a candle: "I am thy lover; if I burn, it is proper. Why dost thou weep?"

The candle replied : "O my poor friend! Love is not thy business. Thou fliest from before a flame; I stand erect until I am entirely consumed. If the fire of love has burned thy wings, regard me, who from head to foot must be destroyed."

Before the night had passed, someone put the candle out, exclaiming: "Such is the end of love!"

Grieve not over the grave of one who lost his life for his friend; be glad of heart, for he was the chosen of Him.

If thou art a lover, wash not thy head of the sickness of love; like Sadi, wash thy hands of selfishness.

A devoted lover holds not back his hand from the object of his affections though arrows and stones may rain upon his head.

Be cautious; if thou goes down to the sea, give thyself up the storm.

CHAPTER IV

Concerning Humility

Thou, O creature of God, waste created of the dust; thcrcforc, bc humblc as thc dust. Bc not covctous, nor oppressive, nor headstrong. Thou art from the dust; be not like fire. When the terrible fire raised his head in pride, the dust prostrated itself in humility.

And since the fire was arrogant and the dust was meek, from the former were the demons formed, and from the latter mankind.

Story of a Raindrop

A raindrop fell from a spring cloud, and, seeing the wide expanse of the sea, was shamed. "Where the sea is," it reflected," where am I? Compared with that, forsooth, I am extinct."

While thus regarding itself with an eye of contempt, an oyster took it to its bosom, and Fate so shaped its course that eventually the raindrop became a famous royal pearl.

It was exalted, for it was humble. Knocking at the door of extinction, it became existent.

Story Illustrative of Pious Men Regarding Themselves with Contempt

A sagacious youth of noble family landed at a seaport of Turkey, and, as he displayed piety and wisdom, his baggage was deposited in a mosque.

One day the priest said to him: “Sweep away the dust and rubbish from the mosque.”

Immediately, the young man went away and no one saw him there again. Thus, did the elder and his followers suppose he did not care to serve.

The next day, a servant of the mosque met him on the road and said: “Thou didst act wrongly in thy perverse judgment. Knowest thou not, O conceited youth, that men are dignified by service?”

Sorrowfully, the youth began to weep. “O soul-cherishing and heart-illuminating friend!” he answered: “I saw no dirt or rubbish in that holy place but mine own corrupt self. Therefore, I retraced my steps, for a mosque is better cleansed from such.”

Humility is the only ritual for a devotee. If thou desire greatness, be humble; no other ladder is there by which to climb.

Story of Sultan Bayazid Bustami[1]

When Bayazid was coming from his bath one morning during the Id festival, someone unwittingly emptied a tray of ashes from a window upon his head. With his face and turban all bespattered, he rubbed his hands in gratitude and said: “I am in truth worthy of the fires of hell; why should I be angered by a few ashes?”

1. Bayazîd Bustami was a celebrated saint of Bustãn, in Persia. He died in A.D. 261.

The great do not regard themselves; look not for godliness in a self-conceited man. Eminence does not consist in outward show and vaunting words, nor dignity in hauteur and pretension.

On the day of Judgment thou wilt see in Paradise him who sought truth and rejected vain pretension.

He who is headstrong and obdurate falleth headlong; if thou desire greatness, abandon pride.

Discourse on Conceit

Expect not him who is possessed of worldly vanities to follow the path of religion, nor look for godliness in him who wallows in conceit.

If thou desire dignity, do not, like the mean, regard the fellows with contemptuous eyes.

Seek no position more honourable than that of being known to the world as a man of laudable character.

Thou deemest him not great who, being of equal rank, is haughtly towards thee; when thou makest a similar display before others, dost thou not appear before them as the arrogant appear before thee?

If thou art eminent, laugh not, if thou art wise, at them that are lowly. Many have fallen from high whose places have been taken by the fallen.

Though thou be free from defect, revile not me who am full of blemishes.

One holds the chain of the Kaba temple in his hands; another lies drunken in the tavern. If God call the latter, who can drive him away? If He expel the former, who can bring him back? The one cannot implore the divine help by reason of his good deeds, nor is the door of repentance closed upon the other.

Story of the Darwesh and the Proud Cadi

A poorly-clad doctor of law and divinity sat one day in the front row of seats in a Cadi's court. The Cadi gave him a sharp look, where upon the usher took the man by the arm and said: "Get up; dost thou not know that the best place is not for such as thee? Either take a lower seat, or remain standing, or leave the court altogether. Be not so bold as to occupy the seat of the great. If thou art humble, pose not as a lion. Not everyone is worthy of the chief seat; honour is proportionate to rank, and rank to merit."

He who sits with honour in a place lower than that of which he is worthy falls not with ignominy from eminence.

Fuming with anger, the doctor moved to a lower seat. Two advocates in the court then entered into a spirited discussion, and flew at each other with their tongues like fighting-cocks with beak and claw. They were involved in a complicated knot which neither could unravel. From the last row of seats the tattered doctor roared out with the voice of a lion in the forest:

"If is not the veins of the neck that should stand out in argument," he said, "but the proofs, which should be full of meaning. I, too, have the faculty of argument."

"Speak on," they answered.

With the quill of eloquence that he possessed, the doctor engraved his words upon the minds of his listeners like inscriptions on a signet-ring; and, drawing his pen through the letters of pretension, he invoked applause from every corner. So hard did he drive the steed of speech that the Cadi lagged behind like an ass in the mire. Removing his cloak and turban, the latter sent them to the doctor as a token of his respect.

"Alas!" he said, "I did not discern thy merit, nor welcome thee on thy arrival. I regret to see thee in the condition with such a stock of knowledge."

The usher then approached the stranger courteously in order that he might place the Cadi's turban upon his head. But the doctor repelled him with his hands and tongue, saying:

"Please not upon my head the fetters of pride, for tomorrow this fifty-yarded turban would turn my head from those in jaded garb. Those who called me 'lord' and 'chief' would then appear insignificant in mine eyes. Is pure water different whether it be contained in a goblet of gold or an earthen ewer? A man's head requires brain and intellect, not an imposing turban like thine. A big head does not make one worthy; it is like the gourd, void of kernel. Be not proud because of thy turban and beard, for the one is cotton and the other grass. One should aim at the degree of eminence that is conformable with one's merit. With all this intellect, I will not call thee man, though a hundred slaves walk behind thee. How well spoke the shell when a greedy fool picked it out of the more: 'None will buy me for the smallest price: be not so insane as to wrap me up in silk.' A man is not better than his fellows by reason of his wealth, for an ass, though covered with a satin cloth, is still an ass."

In this way the clever doctor washed the rancour from his heart with the water of words. Thus do those who are aggrieved speak harshly. Be not idle when thine enemy has fallen. Dash out his brains when thou art able, for delay will efface the grudge from thy mind.

So overcome was the Cadi by his vehemence that he exclaimed, "Verily, thi day is a hard one." He bit his fingers in amazement, and his eyes stared at the doctor like the two stars near the pole of the lesser bear. As for the latter, he went abruptly out and was never seen there again. They in the court clamoured to know whence such an impertinent fellow had come. An official went in search of him, and ran in all directions, asking whether a man of that description had been seen. Some one said: "We know no one in this city so eloquent as Sadi."

A hundred thousand praises to him who said so; see how sweetly he uttered the bitter truth!

Story of the Honey-Seller

A man of smiling countenance sold honey, captivating the hearts of all by his pleasant manner. His customers were as numerous as flies around the sugar-cane—if he had sold poison people would have bought it for honey.

A forbidding-looking man regarded him with envy, being jealous of the way his business prospered. One day he paraded the town with a tray of honey on his head and a scowl on his face. He wandered about crying his wares, but no one evinced desire to buy. At nightfall, having earned no money, he went and sat dejectedly in a corner, with a face as bitter as that of a sinner fearful of retribution.

The wife of one of his neighbours jokingly remarked: "Honey is bitter to one of sour temper."

It is wrong to eat bread at the table of one whose face is as wrinkled with frowns as the cloth on which it is served.

O sir! add not to thine own burdens, for an evil temper brings disaster in its train.

If thou hast not a sweet tongue like Sadi, thou hast neither gold nor silver.

Story Illustrating the Forbearance of Good Men

I have heard that a debased drunkard caught a pious man by the collar. The latter received his blows in silence, and in forbearance lifted not his head.

A passer-by remarked : "Art thou not a man? It is a pity to be patient with this ignorant fellow."

The pious man replied : "Speak not thus to me. A foolish drunkard collars one by the neck in the thought that he is fighting with a lion: there is no fear that a learned man will contend with an inebriated fool."

The virtuous follow this rule in life—when they suffer oppression they display kindness.

Story Illustrating the Noblemindedness of Men

A dog bit the leg of a hermit with such violence that venom dropped from its teeth, and the poor man could not sleep all night through pain.

His little daughter chided him, saying: "Hast thou not teeth as well?"

The unfortunate parent wept, and then smilingly replied: "Dear child! Although I was stronger than the dog, I restrained my anger. Should I receive a sword-blow on the head, I could not apply my teeth to the legs of a dog."

One can revenge oneself upon the mean, but a man cannot act like a dog.

Story of a Kind Master and his Disobedient Slave

An eminent man, famous for his many virtues, possessed a slave of evil disposition, who in ugliness of feature surpassed everyone in the city. He closely attended his master at meal-times, but he would not have given a drop of water to a dying man. Neither reproof nor the rod influenced him; the house was in a constant state of disorder through him. Sometimes, in his bad temper, would he litter the paths with thorns and rubbish; at other times, throw the chickens down the well. His unhappy temperament was written on his face, and never did he perform a task successfully.

Someone asked his master : "What is there that thou likest in this slave—his agreeable manners, or his skill, or beauty? Surely, it is not worth while to keep such an unruly knave and burden thyself with such an affliction. I will procure for thee a slave of handsome appearance and good character. Take this one to the slave-market and sell him. If a piece is offered for him, do not refuse it, for he would be dear at that."

The good natured man smiled and said: "O friend! although the character of my slave is certainly bad, my character is improved by him, for when I have learned to tolerate his manner I shall be able to put up with anything at the hands of others. It were not humane to sell him and thus make known his faults. And it is better to endure his affliction myself than to pass him on to others."

Accept for thyself what thou wouldst accept for others. If distressed thyself, involve not thy fellows.

Forbearance is at first like poison, but when engrained in the nature it becomes like honey.

Story of Maruf Karkhi[1] and the Sick Traveller

No one follows the path of Maruf Karkhi who does not first banish the idea of fame from his head.

A traveller once came to Maruf's house at the point of death—his life was joined to his body by a

---

1. Abul Mahfuz, surnamed Maruf, was a celebrated saint of Kareh, a village in Baghdad. He was the son of a fireworshipper, and was born A.D. 813, during the reign of Caliph Mamun, son of the celebrated Hãrûn-ar-Rashîd.

single hair. He passed the night in wailing and lamentation, sleeping not himself nor permitting anyone else to sleep by reason of his groans. His mind was distressed and his temper was vile; though he died not himself, he killed many by his fretting. Such was his restlessness that everyone flew from him. Maruf Karkhi alone remained. He, like a brave man, girt his loins and sat up many nights in attendance at the sick man's bedside. But one night Maruf was attacked by sleep—how long can a sleepless man kept up?

As soon as the invalid saw him asleep he began to rave : "Cursed be thy abominable race", he cried: "what knows this glutton, intoxicated with sleep, of the helpless man who has one closed his eyes?"

Maruf took no notice of these words, but one of the women of the harem, overhearing them, remarked: "Didst, thou not hear what that wailing beggar said? Turn him out, and tell him to take his abuse with him and die elsewhere. Kindness and compassion have their occasions, but to do good to the evil is evil; only a fool plants trees in barren soil. A grateful dog is better than an ungrateful man."

Maruf laughed: "Dear woman," he replied, "be not offended at his ungracious words. If he rave at me through sickness, I am not angered. When thou art strong and well thyself, bear gratefully the burdens of the weak. If thou cherish the tree of kindness, thou wilt assuredly eat of the fruits of a good name."

They attain to dignity who rid themselves of arrogance.

He who worships grandeur is the slave of pride; he knows not that greatness consists in meekness.

Story Illustrating the Folly of the Ignoble

An impudent fellow begged of a pious man, but the latter had no money in his house. Otherwise, would he have showered gold upon him like dust. The infamous rascal, therefore, went out and began to abuse him in the street.

The eye of the fault-finder sees no merits. What regard has he who has acted dishonourably for the honour of another?

Being informed of his words, the pious man smiled and said: "It is well; this man has enumerated only a few of my bad qualities—only one out of a hundred that are known to me. The evil that he has supposed in me I know for certain that I possess. Only one year has he been acquainted with me; how can he know the faults of seventy years? None but the Omniscient knows my faults better than myself. Never have I known one who has attributed to me so few defects. If he bear witness against me in the Day of Judgment, I shall have no fear. If he who thinks ill of me seek to reveal my faults, tell him to come and take the record from me."

Be humble when the veil is torn from off thy character. If a pitcher were made of the dust of men, calumnious would shatter it with stones.

Story of One Who had a Little Knowledge

A certain man knew something of astronomy and his head, in consequence, was filled with pride. Journeying far, he visited Kushyar,[1] the sage, who turned his eyes from him and would teach him nothing. When the disappointed traveller was on the point of leaving, Kushyar addressed him with these words:

"Thou imaginest that thou art full of knowledge. How can a vessel that is full receive of more? Rid thyself of thy pretensions, so that thou mayest be filled. Being full of vanity, thou goest empty."

Story Illustrating the Humility of the Pious

Someone heard the barking of a dog in the ruined hut of a pious man. Reflecting upon the strangeness of the fact, he went and searched, but found no traces of a dog. In truth, the devotee alone was in the house.

Not wishing his curiosity to be revealed, the man was departing, when the owner of the house cried out: "Come in; why standest thou upon the door? Knowest thou not, O friend, that I it was who barked? When I discerned that humility was acceptable to God, I banished pride and vanity from my heart, and clamoured with barks at the door of God, for I saw none more lowly than a dog."

If thou desire to attain to dignity, let humility be thy path.

---

1. Abû-al Hasan Kûshyãr was a celebrated astronomer and the tutor of Avicenna.

Behold, when the dew lies low upon the earth, the sun doth raise it to the skies.

Story Illustrating the Value of Soft Words

The slave of a king escaped, and, though a search was made, was no discovered. Later, when the fugitive returned, the king, in anger, ordered that he should be put to death.

When the executioner brought out his scimitar, like the tongue of a thirsty man, the despondent slave cried out:

"O God! I forgive the king the shedding of my blood, for I have ever enjoyed his bounty and shared in his prosperity. Let him not suffer for this deed on the Day of Judgment, to the delight of his enemies."

When the king heard these words his anger was appeased, and he appointed the slave to be an officer of the standard.

The moral of this story is that soft speech acts like water on the fires of wrath. Do not the soldiers on the battlefield wear armour consisting of a hundred folds of silk?

O friend! be humble when thou dealest with a fierce foe, for gentleness will blunt the sharpest sword.

Story Illustrating the Wisdom of Feigning Deafness

Many writers affirm the falsity of the idea that Hatim was deaf.

One morning his attention was attracted by the buzzing of a fly, which had become ensnared in a spider's web. "O thou," he observed, "who art fettered by thine own avarice, be patient. Wherever there be a tempting bait, huntsman and snare are close at hand."

One of his disciples remarked: "Strange it is that thou coldest hear the buzzing of a fly that hardly reached our ears. No longer can they call tee deaf."

The Sheikh replied: "Deafness is better than the hearing of idle words. Those that sit with me in private are prone to conceal my faults and parade my virtues; thus, do they make me vain. I feign deafness that I may be spared their flattery. When my assumed affliction has become know not them they will speak freely of that which is good and bad in me; then, being grieved at the recital of my faults, I shall abstain from evil."

Go not down a well by a rope of praise. Be deaf, like Hatim, and listen to the words of them that slander thee.

Story Illustrating for Bearance For the Sake of Friends

A certain man, whose heart was as pure as Sadi's, fell in love. Although taunted by his enemies in consequence, he showed no anger.

Someone asked him:" Hast thou no sense of shame? Art thou not sensible to these indignities? It is abject to expose oneself to ridicule, and weak to endure patiently the scoffs of enemies. To overlook the errors of the ignorant is wrong, lest it be said that thou hast neither strength nor courage."

How elegantly did the distracted lover make reply! His words are worthy to be writ in letters of gold:

"Alone is my heart there dwelleth affection for my loved, thus, it contains no room for malice."

Story of Luqman,[1] the Sage

I have heard that Luqman was of dark complexion and careless of his appearance. Someone mistook him for a slave, and employed him in digging trenches at Baghdad. Thus he continued for a year, no one suspecting who he was. When the truth was known the master was a feared, and fell at Luqman's feet, offering excuses.

The sage smiled and said: "Of what use are these apologies? For a year my heart has bled through thine oppression. How can I forget that in one hour? But I forgive thee, good man, for thy gain has caused to me no loss. Thou hast built thy house; my wisdom and knowledge have increased. I, too, possess a slave, and frequently set him to arduous labour. Never more, when I remember the hardships of my toil, will I afflict him."

He who was not suffered at the hands of the strong grieves not at the frailness of the weak.

If thou be sorrowed by those above thee, be not harsh with thine inferiors.

---

1. Luqman was a famous Greek philosopher, and is supposed by some to have been the author *AEsop's Fables.*

CHAPTER V

Concerning Resignation

Happiness comes from the favour of God, not from the might of the powerful.

If the heavens bestow not fortune, by one valour can it be obtained.

The ant suffers not by reason of its weakness; the tiger eats not by virtue of its strength.

Since the hand reaches to the skies, accept as inevitable the fortune that it brings.

If thy life is destined to be long, no snake or sword will harm thee; when the fated day of death arrives, the antidote will kill thee no less than the poison.

Story of a Soldier of Isfahan

In Isfahan I had a friend who was warlike, spirited, and shrewd. His hands and dagger were for ever stained with blood. The hearts of his enemies were consumed by fear of him; even the tigers stood in awe of him. In battle he was like a sparrow among locusts; in combat, sparrows and men were alike to him. Had he made an attack upon Faridun, he would not have given the latter time to draw his sword. Neither in bravery nor magnanimity had hean equal.

This warrior formed a liking for my company; but as I was destined to remain in Isfahan, Fate transferred me from Iraq to Syria, in which holy land my staying was agreeable. After some time the desire for my home attracted me, so I returned to Iraq.

One night, the memory of the sepoy passed through my mind; the salt of his friendship opened the wounds of my gratitude, for I had eaten salt from his hand. To meet him, I went to Isfahan, and inquired as to where he lived.

I chanced upon him. He who had been a youth had become old; his form, once erect as an arrow, had become as a bow. Like a hoary mountain, his head was covered with snowy hair. Time had conquered him and twisted the wrist of his bravery. The pride of his strength had gone; the head of weakness was upon his knees.

"O tiger-seizer!" I exclaimed, "what has made thee decrepit like an old fox?"

He laughed and said: "Since the day of the battle of Tartary. I have expelled the thoughts of fighting from my head. Then did I see the earth arrayed with spears like a forest or reeds. I raised like smoke the dust of conflict; but when Fortune does not favour, of what avail is fury? I am one who, in combat, could take with a spear a ring from the palm of the hand; but, as my star did not befriend me, they encircled me as with a ring. I seized the opportunity of flight, for only a fool strives with Fate. How could my helmet and cuirass aid me when my bright star favoured me not? When the key of victory is not in the hand, no one can break open the door of conquest with his arms.

"The enemy were a pack of leopards, and as strong as elephants. The heads of the heroes were encased in iron, as were also the hoofs of the horses. We urged on our Arab steeds like a cloud, and when the two armies encountered each other thou wouldst have said they had struck the sky down to the earth. From the raining of arrows, that descended like hail, the storm of death arose in every corner. Not one of our troops came out of the battle but his cuirass was soaked with blood. Not that our swords were blunt—it was the vengeance of stars of ill fortune. Overpowered, we surrendered, like a fish which, though protected by scales, is caught by the hook in the bait. Since Fortune averted her face, useless was our shield against the arrows of Fate."

Story of the Doctor and the Villager

One night a villager could not sleep owing to a pain in his side. A doctor said: "This pain is caused by his having eaten the leaves of the vine. I shall be astonished if he lasts through the night, for the arrows of a Tartar in his breast were better for him than the eating of such indigestible food."

That night the doctor died; forty years have since passed, and the villager yet lives.

Story of the Villager and his Ass

The ass of a villager died, so he set the head upon a vine in his garden in order that it might ward off the Evil Eye.

A sage old man passed by and laughingly remarked: "Dost think, O friend, this will effect the purpose? In life, the ass could not protect itself from blows; so, in weakness, did it die."

What knows the physician of the condition of the sick, when, helpless, he himself will die through illness?

Story Illustrating Luck

A poor man dropped a dinar in the road. He searched much, but at last, despairing, abandoned the attempt.

Someone came along and found the coin by chance.

Good and ill fortune are predestined. Our daily portion depends not upon our strength and efforts, for those who are strongest and strive the most stand often in the direst need.

Story of one Who Blamed His Destiny

There was once a rich and prosperous man named Bakhtyar. The wife of one of his neighbours, who was in the other extreme of poverty, upbraided her husband one night when he went to her empty-handed, saying: "No one is so poor and unfortunate as thee. Take a lesson from thy neighbours, who are well to-do. Why art thou not fortunate like them?"

The man replied: "I am incapable of aught; quarrel not with Fate. I have not been endowed with the power to make myself a Bakhtyar.[1]

---

1. Bakhtyar literally means "fortunate" the play on the word is, therefore, obvious.

Story of a Darwesh and his Wife

A Darwesh remarked to his wife, who was of ill-favoured countenance: "Since Fate has made thee ugly, do not encrust thy face with cosmetics."

Who can attain good fortune by force! Who, with collyrium, can make the blind to see?

Not one among the philosophers of Greece or Rome could produce honey from the thorn.

Wild beasts cannot become men; education is wasted upon them.

A mirror can be freed from stain, but it cannot be made from a stone.

Roses do not blossom on the branches of the willow; hot baths never yet made an Ethiop white.

Since one cannot escape the arrows of Fate, resignation is the only shield.

Story of a Vulture and a Kite

A vulture said to a kite: "No one can see so far as I."

"Possibly," replied the kite; "but what can't thou see across the desert?"

Gazing down, the vulture exclaimed: "Yonder do I see again or wheat."

Thereupon, they flew to the ground. When the vulture settled upon the wheat he became caught in a trap. He had not known that, through his eating the grain, Fate would ensnare him by the neck.

Not every oyster contains a pearl; not every archer hits the target.

"Of what use," the kite inquired, "was it to see the grain when thou couldest not discern the trap of thine enemy?"

"Caution," said the captive vulture, "availeth not with Destiny."

When the decrees of past eternity are brought to action, the keenest eyes are rendered blind by Fate.

In the ocean, where no shore-line appears, the swimmer strives in vain.

Story of a Camel

A young camel said to its mother: "After thou hast made a journey, rest awhile."

"If the bridle were in my hands," was the reply, '"no one would ever see me in the string of camels with a load upon my back."

Fate is the helmsman of the ship of life, no matter though the owner rend his clothes.

O Sadi! look not for aid from any man. God is the giver, and He alone. If thou worship Him, the door of His mercy sufficeth thee; if He drive thee away, no one will ease thee. If He make thee to wear a crown, raise thy head; if not, bot thy head in despair.

Discourse Concerning Hypocrisy

Who knows that thou are not pledged to God even though thou standest in prayer without ablution?

That prayer is the key to hell which thou performest only before the eyes of men.

If the high-road of thy life lead to aught but God, thy prayer-mat will be thrown into the fire.

He whose heart is good and makes no outward show of piety is better than one of outward sanctity whose heart is false.

A night-prowling robber is better than a sinner in the tunic of a saint.

Except not wages from Omar, O son, when thou workest in the house of Zaid.

If in private I am bad and mean, of what avail is it to pose before the world with honour? How much will the bag of hypocrisy weight in the Scales of Justice?

The outside of the hypocrite's coat is neater than the lining, for the one is seen and the other is hidden.

CHAPTER VI

Concerning Contentment

He knows not God nor performs His worship who is not contented with his lot.

Contentment maketh a man rich—tell this to the avaricious.

O irresolute one! be tranquil, for grass grows not upon revolving stones.

Pamper not thy body if thou be a man of sense, for in so doing dost thou seek thine own destruction.

The wise acquire virtue, and they that pamper their bodies are devoid of merit.

Eating and sleeping is the creed of animals; to adopt it is the manner of fools.

Happy is that fortunate man who, in meditation, prepares for the last journey by means of the knowledge of God.

To him who knows not the darkness from the light the face of a demon is as that of a Houri.[1]

How can the falcon fly to the sky when the stone of avarice is tied to its wing?

If thou pay less attention to thy food than to worship thou mayest become an Angel. First cultivate

---

1. "Darkness" and "light" are used metaphorically in the sense of "falseness" and "truth."

the qualities of a man, then reflect upon the character of angels.

Eat in proportion to thy hunger; how can he give praises who scarce can breathe by reason of his gluttony?

He whose stomach is full is void of wisdom. The prey is entrapped in the snare because of its greed.

Story of the King Khwarazm[1]

A covetous man paid an early morning visit to the king of Khwarazm, and twice prostrated himself to the ground before him.

"Tell me, O father," his son inquired, "didst thou not say that Makkah was thy place of worship? Why didst thou today repeat thy prayers before the king?

Contentment exalteth the head; that which is full of avarice comes no higher than the shoulder.

He who has wrapped up the volume of his avarice needs not to write to any one, "I am thy slave and servant."

By begging wilt thou be driven from every assembly; drive it from thyself, so that no one may drive thee away.

Concerning the Evil of Over-eating

Some said to a pious man who was stricken with fever; "Ask for some conserve of roses from such a one."

---

1. Khawãrazm is situated to the east of the Caspian Sea, near the mouth of the Oxus.

"Oh friend!" he replied, "it were better to die in bitterness than to endure the affliction of his sour face."

A wise man does not eat conserve of roses from the hand of one whose face has been soured by pride.

Pursue not that which thy heart desires, for the pampering of the body destroys the fires of life.

The gluttonous man bears the weight of his corpulence; if he obtain not food, he bears the weight of grief. It is better that the stomach should be empty than the mind.

Story of a Glutton

In company with some religious mendicants I entered a date-grove in Busra. One of the party was a glutton. He, having girt his loins, climbed up a tree, and, falling headlong, died.

The headsman of the village asked, "Why killed this man?"

"Go softly, friend," I answered; "he fell from a branch—'twas the weight of his stomach.

Story of a Recluse

The Amir of Tartary presented a silken robe to an elderly recluse, who, putting it on, kissed the hand of the messenger, and said: "A thousand praises to the king! Excellent is this splendid robe, but I prefer my own patched habit."

If thou hast relinquished the world, sleep upon the bare ground—kiss it not before anyone for the sake of a costly carpet.

Story Illustrating the Evil of Avarice

To a poor man who had naught to eat but bread and onions, a foolish man remarked: "Go, wretched man, and bring some cooked meat from the public feast. Ask boldly and be not afraid of anyone, for he who is modest must go without his share."

Acting on this advice, the beggar put on his cloak and started off. The servants of the feast tore off his clothes and broke his arm.

Weeping, he cried: "Oh my soul! What remedy is there for one's own actins? One seized by avarice becomes the seeker of his own misfortunes. After this, the bread and onions are good enough for me."

A barley loaf procured by the exertions of one's own arm is better than a loaf of flour from the table of the liberal."

Story of an Ambitious Cat

A cat who lived in the house of an old woman of humble circumstances wandered to the palace of a noble, whose slaves repulsed the animal with arrows.

Bleeding from many wounds, the cat ran off in terror, thus reflecting: "Since I have escaped from the hands of those slaves, the mice in the ruined hut of the old woman are good enough for me."

Honey is not worth the price of a sting; better it is to be content with the syrup of dates than expose oneself to that.

God is not pleased with him who is not contented with his lot.

Story of a Short-sighted Man and his High-minded Wife

A certain child having cut its teeth, the father bent his head in anxious thought and said: "How can I obtain the bread and food of which the child will now have need?"

"Be not alarmed," his wife replied, "for until our child shall die, He who gave him teeth will send him bread. A rich man provides for his slave; why should not He who created the slave do likewise? Thou hast not the trust in God that the purchased slave reposes in his master."

I have heard that in olden times stones became silver in the hands of saints. Think not that this is contrary to reason—when thou hast become contented, silver and stones will be as one to thee.

Say to the devotee who worship kings that a king is poorer than a darwesh.

A dinar satisfies a beggar; Faridun was but half content with the whole of the kingdom of Persia.

A beggar free from care is better off than a troubled king.

The villager and his wife sleep more happily than the king ever did in his palace.

Though one be a king and the other a cotton-carder, when they sleep in death the night of both becomes day.

Wen thou seest a rich man filled with pride, go and give thanks, O thou who art poor, that thou, praise be to God! hast not the power to inflict injury upon anyone.

Story of a Holy Man who Built a House

A holy man built a house as high as his own stature. Someone said to him: "I know thee able to erect a better house than this."

"Enough," he cried, "what need have I of a lofty roof? This that I have built is high enough for a dwelling which I must leave at death."

Set not thy house in the path of a flood,[1] O slave, for never will it be perfected.

Story of a Sheikh who Became King

A certain king died, and having no heir, bequeathed the throne to a venerable Sheikh. When the recluse heard the roar of the drums of empire, he desired no longer the corner of seclusion. He led the army to left and right, and became so strong and valiant that he filled the hearts of the brave with fear.

After he had slain a number of his enemies some others combined together against him and reduced him to such straits in his fortified town that he sent a message to a pious man, saying: "Aid me with thy prayers, for the sword and arrow do not avail."

---

1. *I.e.* in this transient and fleeting world.

The devotee laughed and said: Why did he not content himself with half a loaf and his vigils? Did not the wealth-worshipping Korah[1] know that the treasure of safety lies in the corner of retirement?"

Discourse Concerning Riches

The generous man may attain to perfection although he possess not gold.

Dost think that if a mean man became a Korah his sordid nature would be changed?

If he who trades in liberality obtain not bread, his nature remains yet rich.

Generosity is the soil, and riches the seed that is sown; give, that the root may not be destitute of a branch.

Exert not thyself in the amassing of wealth, for evil is the smell of stagnant watcr; strive, rather, to be generous, for running water becomes a flood.

The miser who falls from position and wealth but seldom stands a second time upon his feet.

If thou be a precious jewel,[2] grieve not, for Time will not pass thee by; it is the brickbat by the wayside that goes unheeded. Shavings of gold that fall from the scissors are searched for with a candle.

---

1. Korah, the cousin of Moses and the proverbial miser of the Easterns.
2. *I.e.* if you possess merit.

CHAPTER VII

Concerning Education

Those who turn the reins of their desires from unlawful things have surpassed Rustam[1] and Sam[2] in valour.

None is so fearful of the enemy as thou, slave of thine own passions.

The earthly body is a city, containing both good and evil; thou art the King and Reason is thy wise minister.

In this city, the headstrong men pursue their trades of avarice and greed; Resignation and Temperance are the citizens of fame and virtue; Lust and Wantonness the thieves and pick-pockets.

When the king shows favour to the wicked, how can the wise remain in peace?

The passions of evil, envy, and hatred are inherent in thee as is the blood of thy veins. If these thine enemies gained in strength they would turn their heads from thy rule and counsel; no resistance do they offer when they see the mailed fist of Reason.

Night-thieves and vagabonds wander not in the places where the patrols guard.

1. A famous hero; the Herucles of the Persians.

2. The grandfather of Rustam, and, like him, a celebrated hero.

The chief who punishes not his enemy is bereft of power by the strength of the latter.

More on this point I will not speak—a word suffices to him who puts into practice what he reads.

Discourse Concerning the Excellence of Taciturnity

Be silent, O thou who knowest many things! For he that speaketh little will be free from reproach on the Day of Judgment.

The man of many words is deaf; no counsel does he heed like silence.

When thou desirest continually to speak thou findest no sweetness in the speech of others.

Those who reflect upon right and wrong are better than triflers with ready answers.

He that speaks little thou dost never see ashamed; a grain of musk is better than a heap of mud.

Beware of the fool whose volume of words is as that of ten men—a hundred arrows shot and each one wide of the target. If thou art wise, shoot one, and that one straight.

Utter not slander before a wall—oft may it happen that behind are listening ears.

Enclose thy secrets within the city walls of thy mind, and beware that none may find the gates of thy city open.

A wise man sews up his mouth; the candle is burned by means of its wick.

Story Concerning the Keeping of Secrets

Takash, king of Persia, imparted a secret to his slaves, adding, "Tell it not to anyone." For a year they kept the secret in their hearts; in one day it became diffused throughout the world.

The king ordered the slaves to be executed. One among them begged for mercy, saying: "Kill not thy slaves, for the fault was thine. Thou didst not dam up that secret when it was a spring; why seek to arrest its course now that it has become a flood?"

Entrust jewels to treasurers, but be the keeper of thine own secrets. Thou hast the power until the word be spoken; then, does it gain mastery over thee.

Speech is a demon confined in the well of the mind: leave it not free on thy palate and tongue. When the genii has escaped from the cage, no stratagem will bring him back.

Story Illustrating the Pact that Silence is Best for Fools

There was once in Egypt a religious mendicant who never opened his mouth in speech. Wise men assembled around him from far and near, like moths around a candle.

One night, he reflected: "Merit is concealed beneath a silent tongue. If I remain thus silent, how will men know that I am learned?"

Therefore he indulged in speech, and his friends and enemies alike found him to be the most ignorant man in Egypt. His followers dispersed and his glory vanished. So he went on a journey and wrote on the wall of a mosque: "Had I but seen myself in the mirror of understanding I should not imprudently have torn the veil from off my mind. Although deformed, I exposed my figure in the thought that I was handsome?"

A little-talker has a high reputation.

Silence is dignity, and the concealer of blemishes.

Express not in haste the thoughts of thy mind, for thou canst reveal them when thou wilt.

The beasts are silent, and men are endowed with speech—idle talkers are worse than the beasts.

Story Illustrating the Folly of Impertinence

In the course of a dispute someone uttered improper words and was, in consequence, seized and nearly throttled. "O thou conceited fellow!" said an experienced man, "if thy mouth had been closed like a bud, thou wouldst not have seen thy skirt torn like a flower."

Dost thou not see that fire is nothing but a flame, which at any moment can be quenched with water?

If a man possess merit, the merit speaks for itself, not the owner of the merit.

If thou hast not the purest musk, claim not to possess it; if thou hast, it makes itself known by its perfume.

Discourse on Slander

Speak no evil concerning the good or the wicked, for thus thou wrongest the former and makest an enemy of the latter.

Know that he who defames another revealeth his own faults.

If thou speak evil of anyone, thou art sinful, even though what thou sayest be true.

Story Concerning the Same Subject

To one who stretched his tongue in slander, a wise man said: "Speak not evil of anyone before me, so that I may not think ill of thee. Although his dignity is lowered, thine own honour is not increase thereby."

Why thieving is better than slandering

Someone said: "Thieving is better than back-biting."

I replied: "That is strange to me. What good seest thou in thieving that thou givest it preference to slander?"

"Thieves," he explained, "live by virtue of their strength and daring. The slanderer sins and reaps nothing."

Sadi and his Envious Class-friend

A fellow-student at Nizamiah displayed malevolence towards me, and I informed my tutor, saying: "Whenever I give more proper answers than he the envious fellow becomes offended."

The professor replied: "The envy of thy friend is not agreeable to thee, but I know not who told thee that back-biting was commendable. If he seeks perdition through the path of envy, thou wilt join him by the path of slander."

Story of Sadi's Childhood

When a child, unable to distinguished between right and wrong, I once resolved to fast, and a certain devout man thus taught me to perform my ablutions and devotions: "First" he said, "repeat the name of God, according to the law of the Prophet; secondly, make a vow; and thirdly, wash the palms of the hands. Then wash thy nose and mouth three times and rub thy front teeth with thy forefinger, for a tooth-brush is forbidden when fasting. After that, throw three handfuls of water upon thy face; then wash thy hands and arms up to the elbows and repeat thy prayers by the telling of beads and the recital of the attributes and praises of God. Lastly, wipe again thy head and wash thy feet—thus end in the name of God."

"No one," added the old man, "knows the form of ablution better than myself. Dost thou not see that the elder of the village has become decrepit?"

Hearing these words, the elder cried; "O impious wretch! Didst thou not say that the use of a tooth-brush was unlawful in fasting?—I suppose, then, that slander is lawful? Before thou settest about a fast, wash first thy mouth of improper words."

Story of a Sufi's rebuke

Some Sufis were sitting together in private, when one of them opened his mouth in slander.

"Didst thou ever make a crusade in Europe?" he was asked.

"Beyond the four walls of my house," he replied, "I have never placed my feet."

"Never have I met so unfortunate a man," observed the questioner. "The infidel remains safe from his enmity, yet a Mussulman escapes not the violence of his tongue."

Concerning Absent Friends

In relation to an absent friend, two things are unlawful. The first is to squander his possession; the second, to speak evil of his name.

Look not for good words from him who mentions the names of men with scorn, for behind thy back he says those things which he said to thee of others.

He only is wise who concerns himself with his own affairs and is in indifferent to the world.

Where Slander is Lawful

Three persons only is it permissible to slander. The first is a tyrannical king who oppresses his subjects; it is lawful to speak of his misdeeds so that people may beware of him. The second is he who is shameless; deem it not a sin to speak ill of such a one, for by his own actions are his faults revealed. The third is he that gives false weight and is a cheat; say what thou knowest of his evil ways.

Tale-bearers Worse than Back-biters

Someone said to a pious man, "Knowest thou what such a one said chancering thee?"

"Silence!" he replied; "it is best not to know what an enemy said. Those who carry the words of an enemy are assuredly worse than the enemy himself. Only they convey the speech of an enemy to a friend who are in agreement with the enemy. Thou art worse than an enemy, for thou revealest what he said in private."

A tale-bearer makes an old strife now; fly as far as thou art able from one who stirs up a dormant quarrel.

To be tied by the feet in a gloomy pit is better than to carry mischief from place to place.

A quarrel is like a fire which the tale-bearer feeds with fuel.

Faridun[1] and is Wise Vazier

Faridun had a vazier who was discerning and of enlightened mind.

Someone went to the king one day and said: "The vazier is thy secret enemy. There is not a person in the kingdom to whom he has not lent out gold and silver on the condition that at the death the loans shall be repaid.

---

1. Faridun was the seventh king of Persia, his reign commencing about 750 B.C. He was the boast of the Persians and a model of every virtue.

Regarding the vazier with threatening mien, the king exclaimed:

"Thou appearest before me in the guise of a friend; why art thou my enemy at heart?"

The vazier kissed the ground as he replied: "I desire, O renowned king, that all the people should be thy well-wishers. Since at thy death they must repay me, they will pray for thy long life from fear of me."

Approving of this explanation, the king increased the dignities of the vazier, while no one was more ill-fated and changed in fortune than the tale-bearer.

It is not compatible with reason to kindle between two men the fire of strife and burn oneself in the flames.

Discourse Concerning Wives

That poor man is a king whose wife is obedient and chaste. Grieve not over the troubles of the day when at night the dispeller of thy sorrows is by thy side.

He has obtained his heart's desire whose beloved is of the same mind as himself.

If, a woman be pure and of kindly speech, regard neither her beauty nor her homeliness.

A woman of good nature is more to be desired than one of beauty, for amiability conceals a multitude of flaws. Beware the illtempered fairy. May heaven grant protection from a bad woman!

Prison is preferable to a house full of frowns; travelling is a joy to him whose house contains a woman of ugly mind.

Close the door of happiness upon that house whence the woman's voice comes louder than her husband's.

If thy wife take the road to the bazar, beat her, or sit thyself like a woman in thy house. Let her eyes be blind in the presence of strangers; when she goeth from thy house, let it be to the grave.

Take a new wife each Spring, O friend, for last year's almanac serves no purpose.

To walk bare-footed is better than to wear tight shoes; the hardships of a journey are better than discord at home.

Discourse on the Training of Sons

If thou desire that thy name should remain, train thy son in knowledge and wisdom, for if he possess to these thou diest obscure, with no one to commemorate thy name.

Teach him a handicraft, though thou be as rich as Korah. Place no hope in the power that thou hast—riches may go from thee.

A bag of silver and gold is emptied; the purse of an artisan remainst filled.

Dost thou not know how Sadi attained to rank? He journeyed not over the plains, nor crossed the seas. In his youth he served under the yoke of the learned:

God granted him distinction in after-life. And it is not long before he who serves obtains command.

A boy who suffers not at the hands of his teacher suffers at the hands of Time.

Make thy son good and independent, so that he may not be beholden to any man.

Protect him from evil associates; and pity him not if he bring ruin and destruction upon himself, for it is better that a vicious son should die before his father.

Sadi rebuked for his Fault-finding

There was a certain young preacher who was learned and intelligent, a man of sanctity and a true worshipper. He was forcible in eloquence and correct in grammar, but his articulation was so faulty that he could not properly repeat the letters of the alphabet.

I said to a holy man: "The youth has not got his front teeth!"

"Speak not thus," he replied. "Thou hast discerned his fault, but thine eyes are closed to his many virtues. Thorns and roses grow together; why regardest thou only the thorns? He who is of bad nature sees nothing in the peacock but its ugly feet."

Expose not the faults of others, for thereby art thou forgetful of thine own failings.

Whether I be good or evil, keep thou silent, for I am the bearer of my own profit and loss, and God is better acquainted with my character than thou.

I seek no reward from thee for my virtues so that I may not be afflicted by thee by reason of my sins.

For every good act God will bestow, not one, but ten rewards. If thou see one virtue in a man, do thou pass over the ten faults that he hath.

Are not all things created the product of the art of God?—Black they are and white, handsome and deformed. Not every eye and eyebrow that thou seest is good: eat the kernel the nut and throw the husk away.

CHAPTER VIII

Concerning Gratitude

I Cannot give thanks to that Friend, for I know of none that are worthy. Every hair of my body is a gift from Him; how could I thank Him for every hair?

Praise be to the munificent Lord, Who from non-existence brought His creatures into being. Who can describe His goodness? All praises are encompassed by His glory.

See how from childhood to old age he has endowed thee with a splendid robe!

He made thee pure; therefore, be pure—unworthy it is to die impured by sin.

Let not the dust remain upon the mirror, for once grown dull it never again will polish.

When thou dost seek to gain the means of life, rely not upon the strength of thine own arms.

O self worshipper! Why lookest thou not to God, Who giveth power to thy hand?

If by thy striving thou dost aught of good, take not the credit to thyself; know it to be by the grace of God.

Thou standest not by thine own strength—from the Invisible art thou sustained each moment.

A Mother's Warning to Her Son

Sorrowed at the conduct of her son, who gave no ear to her advice, a woman brought to him the cradle in which once he slept, and said! "O weak in love and forgetful of the past! Wast thou not a weeping and helpless child, for whom through many nights I sacrificed my sleep? Thou hadst not then the strength thou hast today; thou couldst not ward the flies from off thy body. A tiny insect gave thee pain: today thou excellest amidst the strong. In the grave wilt thou again be thus, unable to repel the onslaughts of an ant. How, when the grave worms eat the marrow of thy brain, wilt thou relight the Lamp of Intellect? Thou art as a blind man who seeth not the way, and knoweth not that a well lies in his path. If thou be grateful for thy sight, 'tis well; if not, then surely art thou blind. Thy tutor gave thee not the power of wisdom; by God was it implanted in thy feature. Had He withheld this gift from thee, truth would have appeared to thee as falsehood."

Discourse Concerning the Art of the most high God

For thee is set the bright moon in the sky by night, the world-illuminating sun by day.

Like a chamberlain, the heavens spread for thee the carpet of the Spring.

The wind and snow, the clouds and rain, the roaring thunder and the lightning glittering as a sword—all are His agents, obedient to His word, nourishing the seed that thou hast planted in the soil.

If thou be athirst, fret not; the clouds bear water upon their shoulders.

From the bee He giveth thee honey, and manna from the wind; fresh dates from the date-treed and the date-tree from a seed.

For thee are the sun and moon and the Pleiades; they are as lanterns upon the roof of thy house.

He bringeth roses from the thorn and musk from a pod; gold from the mine and green leaves from a withered stick.

With His own hands did He paint thine eye and eyebrows—one cannot leave one's bosom friends to strangers.

Omnipotent is He, nourishing the delicate with His many bounties.

Render thanks each moment from thy heart, for gratitude is not the work of the tongue alone.

O God, my heart is blood, mine eyes are sore when I behold thy indescribable gifts.

Discourse Concerning the Condition of the Weak

He knows not the value of a day of pleasure who has not seen adversity. Hard is the winter for the beggar—the rich man heeds it not. If thou art swift of foot, be thankful when thou lookest upon the lame.

What know they of the value of water who dwell upon the banks of the Jayhun? Ask it of them who are parched in the heat of the sun. What cares the Arab by the Tigris for the thirsty ones of the desert?

He knows the value of health who lost his strength in fever. How can the night be long to thee reclining in ease upon thy bed? Think of him who is racked with fever—the sick man knows the tediousness of the night.

At the sound of the drum the master awakens—what knows he how the watchman passed the night?

Story of Tughral, King of Shiraz, and the Hindu Watchman

One night in winter Tughral passed by a Hindu sentinel, who was shivering like the star Canopus in the icy rain. Moved to pity, he said: "Thou shalt have my fur coat. Wait by the terrace and I will send it by the hand of a slave."

On entering his palace he was met by a beautiful slave, at the sight of whom the poor sentinel passed from his mind. The fur coat slipped through the latter's ears; through his ill-luck it never reached his shoulders.

The king slept through the night devoid of care; but what said the chief watchman to him in the morning?—

Perhaps thou didst forget that 'lucky man' when thy hand was upon the bosom of thy slave. By thee the night was spent in tranquillity and joy; what knowest thou how the night has gone with us?"

They with the caravan bend their heads over the cauldron; what care they for them that toil on foot through the desert sand?

Tarry, O active youths, for old and feeble men are with the caravan. Well hast thou slept in the litter while the driver held the nose-string of the camel. What of the desert and mountains? What of the stones and the sand? Ask how it fares with them that lag behind.

Story of a Thief

A thief was arrested by a night-watchman and bound by the hands. Thus, crestfallen and afflicted, he remained. During the night he heard someone cry out in want.

"How long wilt thou bewail thy lot?" he asked. "Go, sleep, O wretched man! give thanks to God that the watchman has not tied thee by the hands."

Bemoan not thine own misfortune when thou seest another more wretched than thyself.

Story of one who was not what he seemed

Someone passed by a pious man whom he took for a Jew, and, therefore, struck him on the neck. The latter bestowed his robe upon the aggressor, who, becoming ashamed, remarked:

"I acted wrongly and thou hast forgiven me. But what occasion is this for a gift?"

"I stood not up in anger," was the reply, "being thankful that I was not a Jew, as thou didst suppose."

Story of a Sage Donkey

One left behind on the road wept, saying, "Who in this desert is more distressed than I?"

A pack-donkey answered: "O senseless man! how long wilt thou bewail the tyranny of fate? Go, and give thanks that, though thou ridest not upon a donkey, thou art not a donkey upon which men ride."

Story illustrating the Evils of Pride

A theologian passed by a drunkard who had fallen by the wayside. Filled with pride at his own piety, he disdained even to regard him.

The young man raised his head and said: "Go, old man, and give thanks that thou art in the Divine favour—misfortune comes from pride. Laugh not when thou seest one in bonds lest thou likewise became involved. After all, is it not within the bounds of possibility that tomorrow thou mayest fall, like me, by the roadside?"

If with a mosque the heavens have befriended thee, revile not them that worship in the fire-temple.

O Mussulman! fold thy hands and render thanks that He has not bound the idolater's thread about thy waist.

Turn to Him who guides the hand of Fate; blindness it is to look for help elsewhere.

Story of Sadi and the Idolaters

At Sumanat[1] I saw an ivory idol. It was set with jewels like the Manat, and nothing more beautiful could have been devised. Caravans from every country brought travellers to its side; the eloquent from every clime made supplication before its lifeless figure.

"Why," I pondered, "does a living being worship an inanimate object?"

To a fire-worshipper, who was a fellow-lodger and friend of mine, I said with gentleness "O Brahmin! I am astonished at the doings of this place. All are infatuated with this feeble form; they are imprisoned in the well of superstition. No power has the idol to move its hands or feet; if thou throw it down, it cannot rise from its place. Dost thou not see that its eyes are of amber?—It were folly to seek faithfulness from the stony-eyed."

The Brahmin was angered at my words; he became my enemy, and informed the idolaters of what I had said. Since to them the crooked road appeared straight, they saw the straight one crooked. Though a man be wise and intelligent, he is a fool in the eyes of the ignorant.

Like a drowning man, I was destitute of help; save in politeness, I saw no remedy. When the fool bears malice towards thee, safety lies in gentleness and resignation.

---

1. A celebrated temple in Guzerat demolished by Sultan Mahmud of Ghazni in A.D. 1024.

Therefore, I praised aloud the chief of the Brahmins, saying: "O old man! expounder of the Asta and Zend! I, too, am pleased with the figure of this idol. Its appearance was strange in my sight—of its nature I have no knowledge. Only recently have I arrived in this place, and a stranger can seldom distinguish between the evil and the good. Devotion by imitation is superstition what reality is there in the form of this idol, for I am foremost among the worshippers?"

The face of the Brahmin glowed with joy as he said: "Thy question is reasonable and thy actions are good—whoever seeks for proofs arrives at his destination. Who but this idol can raise his hands to God? If thou wilt, tarry here tonight, so that tomorrow the mystery of this may become know to thee."

The night was as long as the Day of Judgment; the fire-worshippers around me prayed without ablution. In the morning, they came gain into the temple, and I was sick with anger and confused from lack of sleep. Suddenly, the idol raised its arm; and later, when the crowd had left, the Brahmin looked smilingly towards me, saying:

"I know that now thou wilt have no doubts; truth has become manifest, falsehood remaineth not."

Seeing his ignorance thus increased, I shed hypocritical tears and cried: "I am sorry of what I said."

At the sight of my tears the hearts of the infidels were softened; they ran towards me in service, and led me by the arms to the ivory idol, which was seated upon a golden chair set on a throne of teak. I kissed the hand of the little god—curses upon it and upon its worshippers! For a few days I posed as an infidel and discussed the Zend, like a Brahmin. When I became a guardian of the temple my joy was such that I could scarce control my feelings.

One night, I closed fast the door of the temple and, searching, discovered a screen of jewels and gold that went from the top of the throne to the bottom. Behind this screen the Brahmin high priest was devoutly engaged with the end of a rope in his hand. Then did it become known to me that when the rope was pulled the idol of necessity raised its arm.

Greatly confused at my presence, the Brahmin ran away in haste: I followed in hot pursuit and threw him headlong down a well, for I knew that, if he remained alive, he would seek to shed my blood. When the purpose of an evil man is revealed to thee, pull him up by the roots, otherwise will he not desire that thou shouldst live. The alarm being raised, I fled quickly from the land. When thou settest fire to a forest of canes, beware of the tigers, if thou art wise.

Whenever I supplicate at the shrine of the Knower of Secrets, the Indian puppet comes into my recollection—it throws dust on the pride of mine eyes. I know that I raise my hand, but not by virtue of mine own strength. Men of sanctity stretch not out their hands themselves the Fates invisibly pull the strings.

CHAPTER IX

Concerning Repentance

O thou of whose life seventy years have passed, perhaps thou hast slept in negligence that thy days have been thrown to the winds. Worldly aims hast thou well pursued; no preparations hast thou made for the departure to that world to come.

On the Judgment Day, when the bazar of Paradise will be arrayed, rank will be assigned in accordance with one's deeds.

If thou shouldest take a goodly stock of virtues, in proportion will be thy profit; if thou be bankrupt, thou wilt be ashamed.

If fifty years of thy life have passed, esteem as a precious boon the few that yet remain.

While still thou hast the power of speech, close not thy lips like the dead from the praise of God.

An old man's lament

One night, in the season of youth, several of us young men sat together; we sang like bulbuls and raised a tumult in the street by our mirth.

An old man sat silent, apart; like a filbertnut, his tongue was closed from speech. A youth approached him and said: "O old man! why sittest thou so mournfully in this corner? Come, raise thy head from the collar of grief and join us in our festivity."

Thus did the old man reply: "When the morning breeze blows over the rose-garden, the young trees proudly wave their branches. It becomes not me to mingle in thy company, for the dawn of old age has spread over my cheeks. Thy turn it is to sit at this table of youth; I have washed my hands of youthful pleasures. Time has showered snow upon my crow-like wings; like the bulbul, I could not sport in the garden. Soon will the harvest of my life be reaped; for thee, the new green leaves are bursting. The bloom has faded from my garden; who makes a nosegay from withered flowers? I must weep, like a child, in shame for my sins, but cannot emulate his pleasures."

Well has Luqman said: "It is better not to live at all than to live many years in sinfulness." Better, too, may it be to close the shop in the morning than to sell the stock at a loss.

Advice and Warning

Today, O youth, take the path of worship, for tomorrow comes old age. Leisure thou hast, and strength—strike the ball when the field is wide.[1]

I knew not the value of life's day till now that I have lost it.

How can an old ass strive beneath its burden?—go thy way, for thou ridest a swiftpaced horse.

A broken cup that is mended—what will its value be? Now that in carelessness the cup of life has fallen

1. *I.e.* engage in good works while you still have time.

from thy hand, naught remains but to join the pieces.

Negligently hast thou let the pure water go; how canst thou now perform thy ablutions, except with sand?[1]

Sadi's Rebuke from a Camel-driver

One night in the desert of Faid[2] may feet became fettered with sleep. A camel-driver awoke me, saying: "Arise; since thou heedest not the sound of the bell, perhaps thou desirest to be left behind! I, like thee, would sleep awhile, but the desert stretches ahead. How wilt thou reach the journey's end if thou sleepest when the drum of departure beats?"

Happy are they who have prepared their baggage before the beat of the drum! The sleepers by the wayside raise not their heads and the caravan has passed out of sight.

He who was early awake surpassed all on the road; what availed it to awaken when the caravan had gone?

This is the time to sow the seeds of the harvest thou wouldst reap.

Go not bankrupt to the Resurrection, for it availeth not to sit in regret. By means of the stock that thou hast, O son, profit can be acquired; what profit accureth to him who consumeth his stock himself?

---

1. Muhammad commanded that sand should be used for ablution before prayer when water was unobtainable, as is more often than not the case in desert.

2. Name of a village on the road to Makkah.

Strive now, when the water reacheth not beyond thy waist; delay not until the flood has passed over thy head.

Heed the counsel of the wise today, for tomorrow will Nakir[1] question thee with sternness. Esteem as a privilege thy precious soul, for a cage without a bird has no value. Waste not thy time in sorrow and regret, for opportunity is precious and time is a sword.

Story Concerning Sorrow for the Dead.

A certain man died and another rent his clothes in grief. Hearing his cries, a sage exclaimed: "If the dead man possessed the power he would tear his shroud by reason of thy wailing and would say: 'Do not torment thyself on account of my affliction, since a day or two before thee I made ready for the journey. Perhaps thou hast forgotten thine own death, that my decease has made thee so distressed."

When he whose eyes are open to the truth scatters flowers over the dead, his heart burns not for the dead but for himself.

Why dost thou weep over the death of a child? He came pure, and he departed pure.

Tie now the feet of the bird of the soul; tarry not till it has borne the rope from thy hand.

Long hast thou sat in the place of another; soon will another sit in thy place.

---

1. The angel who examines the dead in their graves.

Though thou be a hero or a swordsman, thou wilt carry away nothing but the shroud.

If the wild ass break its halter and wander into the desert its feet become ensnared in the sand. Thou, too, hast strength till thy feet go into the dust of the grave.

Since yesterday has gone and tomorrow has not come, take account of this one moment that now is.

In this garden of the world there is not a cypress that has grown which the wind of death has not uprooted.

Story of a Pious Man and a Gold Brick

A gold brick fell into the hands of a pious man and so turned his head that his enlightened mind became gloomy. He passed the whole night in anxious thought, reflecting: "This treasure will suffice me till the end of my life; no longer shall I have to bend my back before any one in begging. A house will I build, the foundation of which shall be of marble; the rafters of the ceiling shall be of aloe-wood. A special room will I have for my friends, and its door shall lead into a garden-house. Servants shall cook my food, and in ease will I nourish my soul. This coarse woollen bed-cloth has killed me by its roughness; now will I go and spread a carpet."

His imaginings made him crazy; the crab had pierced its claws into his brain. He forsook his prayers and devotions, and neither ate nor slept.

Unable to rest tranquil in one place, he wandered to a plain, with his head confused with the charms of his vain fancies. An old man was kneading mud upon a grave for the purpose of making bricks. Absorbed in thought for a while, the old man said:

"O foolish soul! hearken to my counsel. Why hast thou attached thy mind to that gold brick when one day they will make bricks from thy dust? The mouth of a covetous man is too widely open that it can be closed again by one morsel. Take, O base man, thy hand from off that brick, for the river of thy avarice cannot be dammed up with a brick.

"So negligent hast thou been in the thought of gain and riches that the stock of thy life has become trodden underfoot. The dust of lust has blinded the eyes of thy reason—the simoom of desire has burned the harvest of thy life."

Wipe the antimony of neglect from off thine eyes, for tomorrow wilt thou be reduced to antimony under the dust.

Thy life is a bird, and its name is Breath. When the bird has flown from its cage it cometh not back to captivity.

Be watchful for the world lasts but a moment, and a moment spent with wisdom is better than an age with folly.

Why fix we thus our minds upon this caravanserai? Our friends have departed and we are on the road. After us, the same flowers will bloom in the garden, together will friends still sit.

When thou comest to Shiraz,[1] dost thou not cleanse thyself from the dust of the road?

Soon, O thou polluted with the dust of sin, wilt thou journey to a strange city. Weep, and wash with thy tears thy impurities away.

Moral from an Incident in Sadi's Childhood

I remember that, in the time of my childhood, my father (may God's mercy be upon him every moment!), bought me a gold ring. Soon after, a hawker took the ring from my hand in exchange for a date-fruit.

When a child knows not the value of a ring he will part with it for a sweetmeat. Thou, too, didst not recognise value of life, but indulged thyself in vain pleasures.

On the Day of Judgement, when the good will attain to the highest dignity and mount from the bottommost depths of the earth to the Pleiades, thy head will hang forward in shame, for thy deeds will gather around thee.

O brother! be ashamed of the works of the evil, for ashamed wilt thou be at the Resurrection in the presence of the good.

Story of a Man who Reared a Wolf

Someone reared a wolf-cub, which, when grown in strength, tore its master to pieces. When the man was on the point of death a sage passed by and said: "Didst

---

1. *I.e.* your native land.

thou not know that thou wouldst suffer injury from an enemy thus carefully reared?"

How can we raise our heads from shame when we ate at peace with Satan and at war with God?

Thy friend regards thee not when thou turnest thy face towards the enemy.

He who lives in the house of an enemy deems right estrangement from a friend.

Story of a Cheat

Someone robbed the people of their money by cheating, and whenever he had accomplished one of his nefarious acts he cursed the Evil One, who said:

"Never have I seen such a fool! Thou hast intrigued with me secretly; why, therefore, dost thou raise the sword of enmity against me?"

Alas! that the angels should record against thee iniquities committed by the order of the Evil One!

Go forward when thou seest that the door of peace is open, for suddenly the door of repentance will be closed.

Mach not under a load of sin, O son, for a porter becomes exhausted on the journey.

The Prophet is the Mediator of him who follows the highway of his laws.

A Recollection of Childhood

In the time of my childhood I went out with my father during the Id Festival, and in the tumult of the mob got lost. I cried in fear, when my father suddenly pulled my ear, and said: "Several times did I tell thee not to take thy hand from the skirt of my robe."

A child knows not how to go alone; it is difficult to travel on any road unseen.

Thou, poor man, art as a child in thine endeavour; go, hold the skirt of the virtuous. Sit not with the base, but fasten thy hand to the saddle-straps of the pious.

Go, like Sadi, glean the corn of wisdom so that thou mayest store a harvest of divine knowledge.

Story of One who Burned his Harvest

In the month of July, a certain man stored his grain and set his mind at ease concerning it. One night, he became intoxicated and lighted a fire, which destroyed his harvest.

The next day he sat down to glean the ears of corn, but not a single grain remained in his possession. Seeing him thus afflicted, someone remarked: "If thou didst not wish for this misfortune, thou shouldst not in folly have burned thy harvest."

Thou, whose years have been wasted in iniquity, art he who burns the harvest of his life.

Do not so, O my life! Sow the seeds of religion and justice and throw not to the winds the harvest of a good name.

Knock at the door of forgiveness before thy punishment arrives, for lamentation beneath the lash is of no avail.

Discourse on Repentance

He who supplicates the Deity by night will not be shamed on the Day of Judgment.

If thou art wise, pray for forgiveness in the night for the sins that thou hast committed in the day.

What is thy fear if thou hast made thy peace with God? He closes not the door of forgiveness upon them that supplicate Him.

If thou art a servant of God, raise thy hands in prayer; and if thou be ashamed, weep in sorrow.

No one has stood upon His threshold whose sins the tears of repentance have not washed away.

CHAPTER X

Concerning Prayer

Come, let us raise our hands in prayer, for tomorrow they will be powerless in the dust.

Think not that he who supplicates before the Door of Mercy, which is never shut, will turn away in hopelessness.

O Lord, regard us with compassion, for sin has entered among Thy servants.

O gracious God! by Thy bounty have we been su stained; to Thy gifts and loving kindness have we become habituated.

Since in this life Thou hast ennobled us above all things created, hopc of similar glory have we in the world to come.

O God, humiliate me not by reason of Thy greatness; make me not ashamed by reason of my sins.

Let no one prevail over me, for it is better that I should suffer punishment from Thy hand.

Let is suffice that I am ashamed in Thy presence; make me not ashamed before my fellow men.

If the shadow of Thy mercy fall upon me, mean is the dignity of the sky before mine eyes.

If Thou give to me a crown, I will raise my head: exalt me, so that no one may cast me down.

A Worshipper's Lament

I tremble when I recall the prayer of one distracted in the temple of Makkah. Thus did he lament:

"Throw me not down, for no one will hold my hand to succour me. Whether Thou call me or drive me away, my head has no resting place but Thy threshold. Thou knowest that I am poor and helpless; I am oppressed by my evil passions. Keep me from pollution, and forgive my sins. Close not mine eyes from the face of happiness; bind not my tongue when I recite the creed. Place the lamp of Faith before my way; make my hand short from doing evil. From the sun of Thy goodness one ray suffices, for except in Thy rays I am not seen. Why should I weep because of my condition? If I am weak, my refuge is strong."

Story of an Idolater

A fire-worshipper turned his back upon the world and girt up his loins in the service of an idol. After some years he was overtaken by misfortune and wept at the feet of the idol, saying: "I am afflicted—help me, O idol! I am weary—have pity upon me."

Long did he continue in his lamentation, but no benefit did he derive. How can an idol accomplish the desires of a man when of itself it cannot drive away a fly?

The idolater frowned and said: "O thou, whose feet are bound to error! with folly have I worshipped thee for years. Help me to fulfil my wishes, or I will ask them of God."

While his face was yet besmeared with the dust of the idol's feet, the Almighty fulfilled his object.

A pious man was astonished when he heard this. Then did a voice from heaven speak into his ear, saying: "This old man prayed before the idol, but his prayer was not heard. If at the shrine of God he were likewise spurned, what difference would there be between an idol and Him Who is eternal?"